DISASTERS AND HEROIC RESCUES SERIES

Disasters and Heroic Rescues of
NORTH CAROLINA

Scotti Cohn

INSIDERS' GUIDE®

GUILFORD, CONNECTICUT
AN IMPRINT OF THE GLOBE PEQUOT PRESS

INSIDERS' GUIDE®

Text design by Bill Brown Design

The publisher gratefully acknowledges Tommy Tomlinson and the *Charlotte Observer* for permission to reprint portions of "From Bad to Verse: Snow Brings Out Poet in a Parka."

Library of Congress Cataloging-in-Publication Data
Cohn, Scotti.
    Disasters and Heroic Rescues of North Carolina / Scotti Cohn.—1st ed.
        p. cm.
    Includes bibliographical references and index.
    ISBN 0-7627-3704-2 (alk. paper)
    1. Natural disasters—North Carolina. 2. Disasters—North Carolina.
3. Rescues—North Carolina. I. Title.
    GB5010.C63 2005   06 - 735
    975.6—dc22   INSIDER'S GUIDE
                            (AMAZON)
                            6/06 $13.95   2005009943

Manufactured in the United States of America
First Edition/First Printing

*To Ryan and Anne, who will always remember
the Charlotte snowstorm of 2004,
and to the heroes—sung and unsung—
of the Old North State*

Contents

Acknowledgments

My heartfelt gratitude goes to everyone who helped with the creation of this book. In particular, I thank my editors, Laura Strom and Amy Paradysz; Fay Byrd (Wilkes Community College); Jerry Carroll (Forsyth County Public Library); Steve Case (State Library of North Carolina); Bruce Daws (Historic Properties Manager, Fayetteville); Stephen Fletcher (University of North Carolina at Chapel Hill); Carol Ann Freeman (former Public Relations Director, Highland Hospital, Asheville); J. C., Johnny, and Andy Greene (Deep Gap); Philip Hoffman (the *Charlotte Observer*); Wanda Hunter (Cumberland County Public Library); Steve Massengill (North Carolina State Archives); Molly Rawls (Forsyth County Public Library); Joel Reese (Iredell County Public Library); Zoe Rhine (Pack Memorial Library, Asheville); Mary Robinson (Buffalo Bill Historical Center); Michael W. Savchak (Atlantic Coast Railway enthusiast); Bonnie Spiers (State Library of North Carolina); Larry Tew (Cumberland County Historical Society); Susan Robbins Watson (American Red Cross); Peter Wilkerson (University of North Carolina at Asheville); Jeanette Wilson (Lexington Library); Paul Wilson (Methodist College, Fayetteville); and Ann Wright (Pack Memorial Library, Asheville).

Introduction

Shortly after I started researching material for this book, I spoke to a librarian at one of North Carolina's public libraries. I mentioned several of the disasters I planned to cover in the book. After a moment of silence, she remarked, "Oh dear, we sound rather accident prone!" I assured her that the book was part of a series that will include many other states. She seemed relieved to know that North Carolina had not been singled out as a "disastrous" place to live.

The truth is, of course, that disasters can occur anywhere. Natural disasters such as tornadoes, hurricanes, earthquakes, blizzards, and floods strike worldwide, as do train wrecks, mine collapses, disasters at sea, plane crashes, and other man-made catastrophes.

Shipwrecks were a common occurrence in North Carolina's early history. Entire books have been written about the state's treacherous coastal waters—aptly nicknamed the "Graveyard of the Atlantic." Hurricanes not only ravage the coast but cause repercussions inland in the form of heavy rains. In September 2004, even as I was writing a chapter for this book about the July 1916 floods, four hurricanes hit the East Coast. Extensive flooding occurred in the western part of the state, particularly the Asheville area. Pictures of the devastation bore a disheartening resemblance to those taken in 1916 in the same region.

Fortunately, when disaster strikes, people of all ages in all walks of life respond, often heroically. This book focuses on such individuals as well as on the experiences of those they sought to rescue. From the fire that destroyed Fayetteville in 1831 to the snowstorm that slammed Charlotte in 2004, these stories convey what was at stake and what remained after the wind, waves, snow, flames, or smoke cleared. My intention is to show how the people of the Tarheel state have overcome trials and tragedies with profound compassion, selfless courage, and exceptional fortitude.

CHAPTER 1

Fayetteville Is No More

THE GREAT FIRE
— 1831 —

IN 1831 FAYETTEVILLE WAS A PROSPEROUS TOWN OF about 3,000 people. Named after the Marquis de LaFayette, the French general who served in the American forces during the Revolutionary War, Fayetteville was proud of its connection to France. In March 1825 the marquis had visited the town. A grand ball was held in his honor at the LaFayette Hotel.

Fayetteville's location on the banks of the Cape Fear River made it a major eastern North Carolina trade center. The city's appeal and

A woodcut done in 1814 by Horace Say depicts downtown Fayetteville prior to the Great Fire of 1831. North Carolina Collection, University of North Carolina Library at Chapel Hill

functionality were enhanced by two fast-moving creeks that emptied into the river.

Late spring and early summer were especially beautiful in Fayetteville. Along Maiden Lane and Old Street, coralbells bloomed pink and scarlet. A warm breeze carried the fragrance of roses all through the town, from the Cool Spring Tavern to the Mansion Hotel to the little Catholic chapel near Liberty Point. On the morning of May 29, 1831, a dazzling sunrise tinted the sky orange-gold. Chickadees chirped brightly in the dewy air. A perfect Sunday was in the making.

By that afternoon, however, perfection was not even a remote possibility. The noise of crackling flames and explosions replaced birdsong; fire and smoke obscured the sky.

Fayetteville's church bells had just tolled the end of Sunday services when the shouting began: "Fire! There's a fire at the corner of Market Square!"

The Reverend Henry Rowland, recently elected pastor of the First Presbyterian Church, had just conducted morning worship. Rowland was alarmed when he heard the cries. He had witnessed more than one city fire in his life, and he knew what could happen. Not only were most structures built of wood, they were so close together that sparks quickly jumped from roof to roof, and flames could soon rage out of control.

"The engines!" someone yelled. "Get the engines!"

People came running from every part of town. In spite of his concern, Rowland held out hope. Firefighting techniques had improved over the years. These days, men no longer had to carry ladders and other equipment over their shoulders. Fayetteville had pumping carts that a team of men could pull to the scene. In addition, most residents had leather buckets left over from a time when a bucket brigade was the only means available to fight a fire. The whole community would join forces to extinguish the blaze.

Unfortunately, on May 29 in Fayetteville, efforts to limit the damage were ineffective. The fire had started in the kitchen of James Kyle, and in minutes buildings next to the Kyle home were burning. Soon torrents of flame poured in all directions. The roaring inferno coursed down Hay Street past Old Street, then expanded backward in a northern direction to the edge of Cross Creek. The ashes of prized possessions and the acrid smell of burning buildings filled the air.

In Rowland's words, "The engines were burnt at their stands. . . . In less than one hour and a half, our village was literally a sea of flame."

Horses screamed in terror and threw their riders or galloped madly down the street dragging buggies behind them. Many people tossed their belongings out their windows. Some gathered books, valuable papers, money, and furniture and carried them to a safer location. Sadly, there was no "safer location." The conflagration pursued them, driving them from place to place until they finally gave up, abandoning their possessions. Pinewood buildings and wooden warehouses were consumed in no time at all. Rowland watched in horror as the tall steeple of the Presbyterian church became a pyramid of fire.

"For a while it stood firm," he wrote later. "Soon the bell descended with a crash—the steeple trembled, tottered and fell. The Episcopal church, which apparently caught at the same time, was soon in ashes."

James Seawell's residence was next in line. As the wall of flame bore down on it, a small group fought the fire with water and blankets. The wind changed just in time, and the home was spared. With equal courage and perseverance, citizens saved the house of T. L. Hybart and a store belonging to William McIntyre. Not as fortunate were Mr. Eccles's mill, store, and dwelling and a bridge the city had erected just a few years before.

An unknown artist used the image of the Statehouse from a Horace Say woodcut as the model for a depiction of the Great Fire of 1831. Undated artwork courtesy of the North Carolina Office of Archives and History, Raleigh, North Carolina

Many of the stores that caught fire contained gun powder and alcoholic spirits. The resulting explosions threw shingles in every direction, transmitting the fire to distant structures.

Choking on smoke and seared by the heat, townspeople stared in disbelief and dread as St. Patrick's Catholic Chapel, the LaFayette and Mansion Hotels, and the Cape Fear Bank met fiery deaths. Down tumbled the State House, where the North Carolina General Assembly had voted to ratify the United States Constitution back in 1789.

Describing the scene during the fire, Rowland later wrote, "My heart sunk within me. The sick were borne out of their houses, and were lying on pallets in the street. Others, faint and exhausted, were reclining on the beds which had been thrown out. On every side was heard the thunder and the shock of buildings which were blown to pieces."

Desperate, the men battling the blaze had resorted to blowing up buildings in the path of the flames. This was a common technique employed to stop a fire's progress. Many homes and businesses were sacrificed. No one had the energy to remove the shattered timbers from the demolished structures. The crowd could only retreat and wait for the fire to run out of fuel.

Rowland tramped along the outskirts of the inferno, trying to help wherever he could. By 6 P.M., the raging beast had reduced Fayetteville to smoldering ruins. Rowland remained with the masses huddled on the outskirts of town. Children came to him, crying for their parents. Anxious parents asked if he had seen their children.

"The impression made on our hearts is indescribable;" he wrote, "despair seems to reign in every countenance. Not a tear is shed; the horror stricken feelings of our poor sufferers have not yielded to tears."

Exhausted and in shock, people had nowhere to lay their heads. Not even their clothing had been saved. Those who were sick or injured could find no remedy. All the medicine shops and medicine had been destroyed. A few individuals expressed gratitude that this had happened in the spring rather than in winter.

That very evening all were comforted by the announcement that in spite of many severe injuries, no lives had been lost. The residents of Fayetteville had not been able to save their town—more than 600 buildings had been destroyed—but they had managed to save each other.

Although he rejoiced at the news that no one had died, Reverend Rowland realized that simply being alive could not restore the shelter, clothing, and livelihoods the victims had lost to the blaze. Taking pen in hand, he produced a series of letters. To the editor of the *National Gazette,* he wrote: "Sir—FAYETTEVILLE IS NO MORE!—This morning the sun rose upon us in its beauty, and with gladdened hearts we flocked to the churches of our God—now we are in RUINS. . . .

Nothing but stacks of tottering chimneys remain to tell what we once were."

The editors of the *New York Journal of Commerce* received the following comments from Rowland in a letter dated May 30, 1831:

GENTLEMEN—By this time you must have heard that FAYETTEVILLE IS IN ASHES. But two, or at most three stores, at the foot of Haymount, are all that remain standing; all the rest are entirely consumed. . . . It is our hope, that by the blessing of Providence, before the season for the fall business shall arrive, such provision may be made by our merchants for the carrying on of business that, our lives may be sustained so that to the evils of *beggary*, may not be added those of *starvation*.

The citizens of nearby Raleigh acted quickly. In a meeting on May 31, they set up a fund, or "subscription," to which people could donate money "for the relief of the sufferers by the destructive Fire which took place at Fayetteville, on the 29th instant, by which the principal part of the Property of the place was consumed." Nearly $600 was collected on the spot. Raleigh also approved a $1,000 loan for Fayetteville. On June 2 the *Raleigh Register* reported: "For the purpose of relieving their immediate necessities, the Intendant of Police will dispatch to-day or to-morrow several wagons laden with bacon and flour."

As word of the disaster spread, aid began to arrive from all over the country. People in Boston, New York, and Philadelphia donated more than $100,000 from each city. President Andrew Jackson sent $50. On June 18 an article in the *Frederick-Town Herald* of Frederick, Maryland, stated:

Fayetteville having been almost entirely destroyed by fire, whereby hundreds of our fellow citizens have been suddenly and most unexpectedly reduced—some from affluence and many from more than a competency, to a state of want and suffering, with scarcely any of the numerous comforts which so recently surrounded them, it becomes us, not merely to express our sympathies, but to manifest their reality, by promptly affording the relief which is in our power.

The town of Frederick sent $458 to Fayetteville. Meanwhile, the Reverend Jarvis Buxton, pastor of St. John's Episcopal Church, went north to seek aid. He didn't collect just money. Second Presbyterian Church in Troy, New York, donated a bell to replace the one destroyed by the Fayetteville fire. The Boston firemen shipped a fire engine up the Cape Fear River to the afflicted town.

The elders of the Presbyterian Church authorized Reverend Rowland to travel to "many of the principal towns in the northern section of the country" to solicit money, "as no part of the fund contributed to the town could be appropriated to the rebuilding of the church." The funds he collected amounted to a sum almost sufficient to replace the church and session house. St. Patrick's Catholic Chapel also sent representatives north to seek assistance, with much success.

Fayetteville's total loss was estimated at $1.5 million. Thanks to the generosity of citizens from all across America, it was able to begin rebuilding almost immediately. The editors of the *Journal*, Fayetteville's newspaper, printed the following comments on July 7, 1831:

As we pass along the streets of our once beautiful, but now ruinous village, the eye is occasionally cheered and the mind relieved from its melancholy musings, by the appearance of the busy workman, and the usual preparation for building. . . . Each day we have the gratifying assurance that our townsmen do not despair. . . . Two respectable frame houses have been nearly completed, four other frames have been put up, and we are glad to learn that several gentlemen have determined to build a block of brick buildings. . . . We state with pleasure that a handsome new bridge has been thrown over Cross Creek, on Green street, and is nearly finished.

In August 1832 a new Presbyterian church was erected on the walls of the original. The steeple bell, having been damaged in the fire, was replaced by one that bore a Latin inscription that translates: "I perished in the flames the 29th of May, 1831. I arose from the ashes through the generosity of friends in the Second Presbyterian Church, Troy, New York."

In his dedication sermon for the new church, Rowland said:

> As we sit here to enjoy the blessings of this sacred place, we cannot fail to ask, who, amidst the deprivation of our worldly hopes, hath administered to our relief? What hand hath reared from the dust this goodly structure, and reanimated our fallen countenances? It is the kind hand of Christian charity. . . . But in rendering this just tribute to our Christian friends, we are not to forget the goodness of God in the direction of this joyful event.

The LaFayette Hotel was rebuilt across the street from its original location, where it stood until it was destroyed by fire in 1885. The former State House was replaced by the Market House, so named because vendors sold produce and meats under its Moorish arches. The second floor served as the town hall. Two buildings constructed before the fire are still standing: Cool Spring Tavern, built in 1788, and Liberty Point, built between 1791 and 1800.

James Kyle, in whose kitchen the great fire started, contributed greatly to the growth and development of Fayetteville. A house built by his family on Green Street in 1855 is listed in the National Register of Historic Places. Down through the years his descendants have played a major role in the Fayetteville Fire Department.

CHAPTER 2

Remember My Last Words
THE WRECK OF THE STEAM PACKET *HOME*
– *1837* –

THEY CAME FROM AS FAR NORTH AS NEW HAMPSHIRE, as far south as Florida, and from nearly every state in between. The Southerners were headed home; the Northerners were traveling south to visit friends or family. On October 7, 1837, they gathered at the foot of Market Street to board an elegant steam packet, or steamship, called the *Home*.

The Steamship Home *battles a storm off the Outer Banks.* Photo is from *Steamboat Disasters and Railroad Accidents* by S. A. Howland (from the collection of Gary Gentile).

They were students, merchants, politicians, unmarried men and women, husbands, wives, and children. The youngest was an infant; the oldest was seventy. They had one thing in common: All of them were looking for fast, comfortable, safe passage from New York to Charleston.

The *Home* was fast: The wooden-hulled, side-wheel steamer had already set a record by making the voyage from New York to Charleston in sixty-four hours. Most people were confident she would beat her own record on this trip. The *Home* was also comfortable: At 198 feet by 22 feet by 12 feet, she could accommodate 120 people with berths or staterooms. The interior featured mahogany and cherry paneling as well as dazzling skylights, saloons, and lavish passenger quarters.

As for safety, there were those who did not trust any of the steam-driven contraptions that had become all the rage. Boiler explosions on steam locomotives and ships were a little too common. Equally troubling, the voyage to Charleston required passing North Carolina's eastern coast, where warm and cold air currents intersected, often creating destructive, pounding waves. The waters along Cape Hatteras and the Outer Banks had long ago earned the nickname the "Graveyard of the Atlantic." Submerged shoals had been claiming victims since the earliest days of sea travel.

Nevertheless, the *Home*'s excellent credentials inspired confidence. She was built at the highly respected Brown and Bell shipyard under the direction of James P. Allaire, owner of the Southern Steam Packet Company, one of the foremost steam manufacturers of the day. The *Home* had already made two successful ocean voyages, and her captain for the October 7 trip was Carleton White, a man with an excellent reputation.

That was good enough for the ninety people who assembled at the Market Street wharf at 4 P.M. on October 7, eager to be on their way.

Hardy Bryan Croom, his wife Frances, and their three children were headed to their Florida plantation. Originally from North Carolina, Croom had served as a state senator there. He planned to celebrate his fortieth birthday—October 8—aboard the *Home*.

The Reverend George Cowles and his wife, Elizabeth, were looking forward to visiting relatives in Augusta, Georgia. The two were deathly afraid of the open sea, but Reverend Cowles was not in good health. An overland journey through the low countries of the South was risky during the warm months, when disease was at its worst. The couple elected to make the trip by water instead.

One might have expected Phillip and Isaac Cohen of South Carolina to avoid steamships. Just one year earlier, in October 1836, the brothers had barely survived the wreck of the *William Gibbons* when it grounded on a sandbar. Friends had urged them not to book passage on the *Home*, but the Cohens ignored their pleas.

Mary and Oliver Hillhouse Prince were on their way to Athens, Georgia. Mr. Prince had been a member of the Georgia state senate and had served as U.S. senator from Georgia. After four months in Boston and New York, his wife was particularly eager to depart. She was homesick and missed her son, a student in Gwinnett County, Georgia. Back in May, before leaving for the North, she had written a note to him, saying: "My own dear Oliver . . . I had hoped to go & see you before we left but that has been impossible." She closed with: "My son, if I never see you more, remember my last words would be 'Remember your Creator in the days of your youth.'"

Oliver H. Prince Jr. may or may not have wondered about his mother's request. Later he would feel the full impact of her words.

The weather that October afternoon was not ideal. The sky was cloudy at 5 P.M. as the boat left the dock with its ninety passengers and forty-five crew. However, a light wind was blowing, and it seemed likely that the weather would soon clear. The steamboat *Isis* led the

Home through Buttermilk Channel, past Governor's Island. After that the *Home* was on its own, headed for the open sea and a new speed record for the New York–Charleston run.

Unfortunately, Romer Shoal near Sandy Hook got in the way. About an hour and a half out of port, wind and the ebbing tide gently pushed the ship aground. Although the jolt was unpleasant, no one was harmed. Captain White and Captain Alfred Hill, whose wife was a passenger, determined that the *Home* was undamaged. However, they announced that further progress would be delayed until high tide. It was obvious that no speed record would be set on this trip. On the bright side, the travelers did not have to deal with constant swaying and rolling as they ate their evening meal.

Everyone was in good spirits. Mr. Prince conversed at length with Mr. Hussey of Charleston and Reverend Cowles; Professor Nott of Columbia, South Carolina, discussed college life with Mr. Kennedy, a student at Yale; Miss Henrietta Croom chatted with Mrs. Levy of Charleston and her daughters, who had spent the summer in New York. (One of the daughters had been sent North to recover her health, with excellent results.) James B. Allaire, nephew of the *Home*'s owner, elaborated on the ship's finer features at the request of Mr. Tileston and Mr. Vanderzee of New York and Mrs. Boudo of Charleston.

High tide arrived on schedule. Captain White and his crew worked the *Home* free through skillful use of both steam and sail. By 10:30 P.M. the ship was under way again, aided by a moderate breeze.

The following day, Sunday, Mr. Croom celebrated his birthday with his family and newfound friends, including Mr. Anderson of Columbia, Mr. Sprott of Benton, Alabama, and Mrs. Riviere, a successful milliner from Charleston.

At noon the wind picked up and Sunday's lunch was a bit of a challenge. Although many passengers retired to their rooms with seasickness, the ship rode the choppy waves without any apparent diffi-

The Steamship Home *in Charleston Harbor.* Photo is from *Steamboat Disasters and Railroad Accidents* by S. A. Howland (from the collection of Gary Gentile).

culty. Then, at around 7:30 P.M., Captain White received bad news from his chief engineer. A feeder pipe to the forward boiler had opened at the joint. Water was leaking into the hold instead of flowing into the boiler.

Using the remaining boiler and square sail, White steered toward Chesapeake Bay. If the damaged boiler pipe could not be repaired, he would anchor there. To his relief, the necessary repairs were completed by midnight. White headed south-southeast under full steam. He had no way of knowing that the *Home*'s problems were far from over.

Soon a passenger appeared on deck, complaining that water was coming into his berth. He was joined by others with the same complaint as the weather worsened. Daybreak on October 9 found the *Home* fighting gale-force winds and rough seas about 20 miles off Hatteras Island, the longest and easternmost segment of the Outer

Banks. The weather was courtesy of what would later be called Racer's Storm. It had begun as a hurricane off the coast of Jamaica.

At 9 A.M. a leak was discovered in the machinery spaces. The feeder pipe had broken again. The engineer struggled to repair it, this time while monstrous waves washed over the ship, knocking it about like a toy. The paddle wheels rose out of the water repeatedly. Once again Captain White steered for the beach. When he received word that the boiler pipe was fixed, he turned for deeper water.

No food could be prepared or served on the *Home* as it pitched and bucked, but breakfast was the last thing on the passengers' minds. They had begun tearing blankets into strips, knowing they might have to use them to tie their friends and loved ones to any part of the ship sturdy enough to survive the storm. By 2 P.M. panels were falling from the ceiling. The boat was bending and twisting like a reed in the stormy surf.

Reverend Cowles, in feeble health, stayed in his berth. At his request, David Milne, a ship's steward, read aloud to him from the Bible. A small crowd gathered to listen.

Suddenly a huge wave broadsided the ship, shearing off part of the bulkhead. The angry sea rushed into the boiler room and flooded the deck and cabins. As the *Home* passed around the Diamond Shoals, passengers, waiters, and deckhands applied their strength to the hand pumps or bailed water with whatever containers they could find. Reverend Cowles sat on a trunk and passed empty pails to the bucket brigade, which included his wife. Mr. Prince took command of a pump. When he left for a moment to make sure his wife was safe, she urged him to quickly return to his station for everyone's sake.

Andrew Lovegreen of Charleston tolled the ship's bell incessantly, hoping that somehow someone would hear it and send help. In another part of the ship, the elderly Mrs. Lacoste, a large woman who often had difficulty getting around on land, saw only one chance to save her life: She asked someone to tie her to a settee with blanket strips. Other passengers lashed themselves to various parts of the ship.

The darkness grew deeper as night descended. The *Home*'s furnace fires succumbed to the flood. Its tattered sails were no match for the high winds. Just before 11 P.M., the ship ran aground on a sandbar several miles east of Ocracoke Village. One of three lifeboats was smashed by the impact. People leaped into the remaining two boats. One capsized as soon as it hit the churning waves; the other landed upright but immediately sank. The cries of the terrified victims could barely be heard above the relentless howl of the wind.

Although the moon was shrouded by clouds, it was still possible to see land about a hundred yards away. The ship was facing the shore. The remaining passengers were told to go to the bow, or front section, of the boat. A lifeline was passed to them by a crew member, and they were advised to cling to it in a sudden emergency. Mrs. Prince joined the throng. Reverend Cowles shuffled along, his arm around Mrs. Cowles. At that moment a giant breaker rose up, obscuring the view of land. With a deafening crash, the waves slammed over the boat, sweeping Cowles and the others away. There was nothing anyone could do to save them.

Breakers continued to lash the *Home* as if trying to beat it to pieces. They destroyed the smokestack, smashed in the starboard staterooms, and dashed the dining cabin to bits. The mainmast snapped. The spars (poles supporting the sails and rigging), rigging, and canvas tumbled down. Captain Hill, who had survived several shipwrecks, decided that he and his wife should try to reach shore by holding onto one of the spars. Phillip and Isaac Cohen jumped overboard to take their chances in the crazed ocean.

The ship's hull separated from the upper deck, and the sea claimed yet another group of victims. As the *Home* began to come apart before his eyes, Captain White made his way to the forecastle, a section of the upper deck, where he found six men clinging to ropes. The foredeck broke loose, and the men soon found themselves on a makeshift raft, riding the angry surf. Twenty-five minutes had passed since the *Home* hit ground.

The storm raged on as the pounding waves propelled the ship's more fortunate passengers onto the beach. Battered, dazed, and shivering from the cold, a number of them huddled under the lee of a sandhill. A few stalwart souls hiked 6 or 7 miles to a lighthouse. Captain White searched the shore for survivors who might need help.

Come dawn the inhabitants of Ocracoke Village were greeted by a scene that was all too familiar to them: a beach littered with bodies and debris. They brought the living to their houses to care for them, and helped make arrangements for burying the dead. Most of the luggage was lost. The trunks that floated to shore were empty.

On October 10 Captain White wrote a letter to James P. Allaire, owner of the *Home:* "Dear Sir: I have now the painful duty of informing you of the total loss of the steam packet Home, and the lives of most of the passengers and crew. . . . Most of the passengers have lost nearly all their baggage. I have lost everything; having nothing but one pair of pantaloons, and a shirt that I had on when I washed ashore."

In his letter White listed those who had been saved. Among them was Mrs. Lacoste, whose settee had borne her to shore, quite a bit worse for the wear but alive. According to one account, she was washed back into the surf several times before others could get to her and pull her to safety. Mr. Hussey floated in on a spar. Other survivors included Andrew Lovegreen, who had tolled the bell up until the very moment the ship began to fall apart; David Milne, the steward who read the Bible for Reverend Cowles; and Mrs. Schroeder, who was tied to one of the boat's braces. Also alive was Mr. Vanderzee, who had tied Mrs. Schroeder to the brace. After watching with alarm as the brace broke from the ship and carried her away, he was greatly relieved to see her again. Captain Hill was alive, but his wife had lost her hold on their spar and drowned. Isaac Cohen had survived but was badly injured.

In all, twenty crew members and twenty passengers, including one child, survived the wreck of the *Home*. Dead were Phillip Cohen, Reverend and Mrs. Cowles, Mr. and Mrs. Croom and their children, Mr. and Mrs. Prince, Professor Nott and his wife, Mr. Kennedy, Mrs. Levy and her daughters, Mrs. Riviere, Mrs. Boudo, Mr. Sprott, Mr. Tileston, James B. Allaire (nephew of the owner), and seventy-five others.

Down in Gwinnett County, Georgia, Oliver H. Prince Jr. could only reread his mother's last letter to him again and again, dwelling on her prophetic note: "My son, if I never see you more, remember my last words. . . ."

As news spread about the disaster, it was revealed that the *Home* had carried only two life preservers. The two people who used them had made it safely to shore. The United States Congress later required all passenger ships to carry one life preserver for each person onboard and, with the creation of the Steamboat Inspection Service in 1871, steamboat safety improved dramatically. Of course, such reforms were too late for the passengers of the *Home*.

Today all that is left of the elegant steam packet is its boiler, which lies buried 10 feet under the sand on an Ocracoke beach.

CHAPTER 3

Tragedy of Errors

THE WRECK OF
THE *METROPOLIS*
– 1878 –

THE JARRING SOUND COMING FROM THE HOLD WAS
the captain's first warning that the voyage might be doomed. The
Metropolis had left Philadelphia on Tuesday, January 30, 1878, under
fair skies, and had traveled on calm seas all day. Choppy waters and
rough winds had caused a few problems on Wednesday—most of the

This engraving of the Metropolis *from* Frank Leslie's Illustrated Newspaper
shows the ship battling high winds and heavy waves off Currituck Beach on Jan-
uary 31, 1878. Courtesy of The North Carolina State Archives

250 passengers had become seasick, some violently so—but that did not alarm Captain J. H. Ankers. Far more disturbing to him was the harsh grating noise, especially when he found out what was causing it. Every time the ship lurched, her cargo of iron rails shifted, pushing against the seams of the hull—seams that might not tolerate that kind of pressure very well.

Best described as a passenger-freighter, the steamship *Metropolis* was no "floating palace." She boasted no spiral staircases or crystal chandeliers. At 198 feet long, 34 feet across the beam, and 16 feet deep, she was sensible and serviceable. That suited Thomas Collins, co-owner of the P. and T. Collins Company, just fine. His firm was looking for three vessels to transport cargo and passengers from Philadelphia to Brazil. Most of those aboard would be laborers and foremen hired by the National Bolivian Navigation Company to build a railroad. The six-year-old steamship appeared to be the perfect choice.

What Collins did not know was that the *Metropolis* was not quite what she seemed to be. Her owners had lied about her age and altered her papers. They had also neglected to mention a few important details about her history. Originally built for commercial use in 1861 (making her seventeen years old, not six, in 1878), the *Metropolis* had seen action under the name *Stars and Stripes* during the American Civil War. Decommissioned in 1865, she was reconditioned for the freight and passenger trade and christened *Metropolis*. She then served a five-year hitch on the New York–Havana run before being sold to George D. Lunt and his partners in 1871. Those gentlemen lengthened the ship, added more cylinders to her engine, then operated her for six more years between New York and various East Coast, Caribbean, and South American ports.

About a month before Collins engaged the *Metropolis,* the Atlantic Coast Line Railroad had sent her from Norfolk, Virginia, to Wilmington, North Carolina, to pick up a load of cotton. The trip was cut short when water began to fill the engine room. The railroad company canceled the charter, and the ship's owners rushed the *Metropolis* to New York for repairs.

Collins knew the *Metropolis* had recently undergone repairs, but saw no reason to doubt the inspection report, which stated that she was a fit, seaworthy vessel. However, a time would come when he would question everything he had been told.

The first of Collins's three ships, the *Mercedita,* left Philadelphia for Brazil on January 2 with Collins's brother, Philip, aboard. The third ship, the *Richmond,* was scheduled to make the trip in February. On Monday, January 28, the *Metropolis* began boarding. The weather in Philadelphia was not bad. After a low of thirty-six degrees the night before, the temperature reached a high of forty-two, with traces of precipitation.

At Reading Railroad wharf the scene was hectic as friends and family gathered to bid an emotional farewell. The engineers, mechanics, bricklayers, and other skilled workers boarding the *Metropolis* had signed contracts to work in Brazil for three years. Husbands and wives parted reluctantly, dreading such a long separation. Children clung to their fathers and begged to be taken along.

In reference to the large number of Irishmen making the trip, one reporter observed: "The scenes were such as the quays of Queenstown and Londonderry witnessed half a century ago, when the sons of the Green Isle bade tender and tearful farewells to their friends and relatives as they embarked for America."

Meanwhile the ship's 1,000-ton cargo of iron rails, stores, and coal was loaded into the hold. A few days later the manner in which this cargo was loaded would be a topic of heated discussion all across the country.

After laying at anchor all night, the ship pulled out of Philadelphia at 9 A.M. on January 29. While the crew went about their jobs, the more than 200 laborers and 20 saloon passengers, including 3 women, relaxed and discussed whatever was on their minds. Perhaps some of them talked about rumors they had heard concerning a new invention. Less than two months earlier Thomas Edison had demonstrated his tinfoil phonograph, becoming the first person to record and play back the human voice. A leading French scientist had already denounced the demonstration, claiming it was the trick of a clever ventriloquist.

A few of the passengers might have talked about the wreck of the *Huron,* one of the U.S. Navy's new warships. Back in November the *Huron* had run aground at Nag's Head, North Carolina. Ninety-eight officers and enlisted men had died. The ship had been within 2.5 miles of a lifesaving station, but the station had been closed until December, when it would open for the "active season." Fortunately, the *Metropolis* was passing the treacherous Outer Banks in January. Lifesaving stations were more likely to be fully staffed.

The travelers may also have been curious about their final destination. Many probably knew little or nothing about life in South America or the project for which they had been hired. A 180-mile railroad track was being built along the Madeira River in order to circumnavigate impassable rapids and waterfalls. The ultimate goal was to ease the transport of valuable materials such as *cinchona,* also called quinine bark, out of the jungle. Quinine was a proven cure for malaria.

By the time Captain Ankers heard the peculiar grinding sound on Wednesday evening, January 30, the majority of his passengers were too sick to care about much of anything. Besides, there were plenty of other sounds and sensations to distract them. Fitful waves jolted the aging steamer, causing her wooden hull to creak and groan as if in pain. The wind screeched like a banshee in the rigging.

Down in the cargo hold, the captain stared in dismay. The iron rails shifted and pushed against the seams of the hull each time the ship lurched. Suddenly he heard shouting overhead: "Fire! Fire!"

Ankers dashed up to the deck, only to discover that the cries were a false alarm. The next alarm was all too real. First Engineer Jake Mitteager informed him that there was a leak near the rudderpost (the vertical post that allows the rudder to pivot). The water was already waist deep. It was difficult to keep the engines running steadily. "We have to lighten the load," Ankers declared. "Throw some of the coal overboard!"

A call went out for everyone to assemble in the main cabin. A bucket brigade was formed to haul coal up from the storage bins and pass it to the main deck, where it could be thrown over the side of the ship. Some of the laborers participated in spite of being seriously ill. They worked throughout the evening and into the night. Finally, after midnight, the circulating pumps began to regain control of the water. The men collapsed where they stood.

Down below, the iron rails continued to shift. The seams of the hull began to widen, and more water poured in. The pumps broke down again. More passengers joined the bucket brigade. The storm gained strength, and the rain turned to snow. Howling winds tore away the smokestack, several of the lifeboats, the bulkhead, the after-mainsail, and the doors of the forward saloon, letting even more icy water in.

The ship was completely dark. Chief Engineer Joseph Lovell raised a lantern to see what conditions were like in the fire room. He almost wished he hadn't. It was full of water. "We have to try to keep the steam up!" he shouted to the crew. "Help me!"

Together they fed a barrel of tallow to the furnace as well as all the wood they could find. Life preservers were passed out to the terrified passengers. Those who were not too sick helped bail water, passing buckets from one to another and out the hatchways. Their efforts were to no avail. Just before dawn on January 31, the engine fires went out.

Captain Ankers scanned the stormy darkness, desperately seeking a light that might guide him to shore. Soon he spotted the flashing beacon of the Currituck Beach Lighthouse. Ankers knew that grounding the ship was the only hope he had. He ordered the remaining sails set and headed toward the beacon.

Instead of hitting dry land as the captain had wished, the *Metropolis* struck an outer sandbar, washed over it, and finally lodged on an inner bar at about 6:45 A.M. The steamer was only a hundred yards from the beach, but it might as well have been miles away. Huge breakers loomed between ship and shore. Not only that, the turbulent waves tossed pieces of the ship in every direction. Anyone who got into the water risked being struck by wreckage.

Ignoring the hazards, six men launched one of the remaining lifeboats. Three more leaped over the side of the *Metropolis* and began swimming through the bone-chilling surf. Miraculously, they made it to shore and set out in search of help.

The steamer's whistle was no longer working, but the crew tolled the ship's bell constantly, hoping that someone would hear it. At about that time, N. E. K. Jones and Jimmy Capps, both residents of Currituck Beach, happened along. Jones later described what occurred: "After a blow, I generally make it a custom to go out on the beach to see if any vessel or stranded property has come ashore. I, in company with James E. Capps, went out on the beach Thursday morning between 8 and 9 o'clock. While on our way we saw the mast of a vessel."

The two men hurried down to the edge of the water. In the fog and mist, they could not tell whether the ship was intact or if anyone was still onboard. As Jones told it, he "told Capps to go up to Mr. Brock's (the nearest neighbor) and get his horse and go to station four and notify them of the wreck." Station Four was the Jones Hill Station, constructed along with six other lifesaving stations on the North Carolina coast in 1874. The *Metropolis* had run aground between two stations that were 13 miles apart.

Capps immediately headed for Swepson Brock's house, less than a mile away. Meanwhile, Jones pulled men out of the heavy surf as they struggled to shore. All were wearing life preservers, he noted. "It was with difficulty that I could free myself from one of the men I pulled out," he reported later. "He held on to me after I got him out of the water, but I had to leave him and attend to others."

Finding Brock at home, Capps told him about the wreck. Brock saddled his horse and raced to the Jones Hill Station. While the surfmen at the station loaded supplies and equipment into their handcart, Brock and John Chappell, the station keeper, rushed a medicine chest to the scene of the disaster. On the way, they encountered a man and woman who had been washed ashore. Brock and Chappell attempted to revive them but were not successful.

The sequence of events that followed could have been called a "comedy of errors" had there been anything even remotely humorous about the situation. The six men from the Jones Hill Station set out with their cart, which carried about 1,000 pounds of gear. Storm tides had rendered the sand so soft and deep, the cart sank at every step. The men were already tired, having just finished night patrol, which involved hiking up to 32 miles. Pushing and pulling with all their might, they struggled along at a painfully slow pace.

Finally John Dunton approached on his horse. He had been busy finding clothing and food for survivors who had made their way to his house, and was now on his way to the stranded ship. "I rode about one-eighth mile down the beach," he recalled later, "when I overtook the lifesaving crew, station 4, with their hand-cart. . . . They were worn down, it being a bad beach for men to travel, and asked me for assistance. I hitched onto the cart and was glad to do so. I took them down to the wreck."

It had been six hours since the *Metropolis* ran aground.

Once the surfmen arrived at the site, they made two attempts to shoot a line to the ship. One flew over but well beyond it; the other landed onboard but was placed by a crew member in such a way that it scraped against a spar (a pole supporting the sails and rigging) and eventually broke. The lifesavers prepared to fire another shot, only to discover that they were out of powder. A supply was procured from

Swepson Brock's home, but subsequent attempts to get a line to the vessel failed. The mainmast crashed to the deck. The rest of the cabin was torn away. The people on the *Metropolis* were left with only one choice.

"They accepted their last alternative," Captain J. H. Merryman of the Lifesaving Service wrote in his report about the incident, "and singly and sometimes in groups plunged overboard, trusting their lives to the treacherous waves. The surf by this time was running high, and the waters were laden with floating fragments of the wreck, amid which, sorely and in some cases fatally injured, drifting northward and driven by the rolling breakers shoreward, came the struggling, drowning people, to be received in the welcome arms of their rescuers, who, with precarious foot-hold, strove in their work waist-deep in the inner breakers and undertow."

The rescuers included lifesaving personnel, survivors, local residents, and Brock's Newfoundland dog. Finally, when there was nothing left to cling to, Captain Ankers, who had put on a "Merriman suit" (similar to a modern wet suit), began to swim toward land. Surfman Piggott Gillikin saw him coming and later reported that he was "sometimes head up, then feet up; on his face, and sometimes on his back. . . . Keeper caught him first, then I got his right hand, and Mr. Brock got hold of his right shoulder." Not only was the captain exhausted, his rubber suit had somehow filled with water, rendering it worse than useless.

As night fell the last survivors reached shore. By the light of driftwood fires, the ship's doctor, G. D. Green, did what he could for them. Many were taken to nearby homes; some remained huddled around the fire until morning, when outside relief parties arrived.

In Philadelphia businessmen and merchants gathered to set up a fund for the families of the victims. The office of the P. and T. Collins Company was besieged by people begging for news of their loved ones. Thomas Collins could not stop thinking about the fact that he and his wife were supposed to have traveled on the *Metropolis*. At the last minute, however, when they saw how crowded the vessel was, they had decided to postpone their trip until February.

According to official reports, the death toll from the wreck was eighty-five. Survivors suffered from a multitude of illnesses and injuries, including pneumonia, tonsilitis, pleurisy, bruises, cuts, and strained muscles.

Yet life went on. According to the *New York Times*, "Notwithstanding the fate of those on the wrecked steamer, hundreds of men applied to the contractors to-day to fill their places, and notices had to be posted that no applications would be received until Monday."

The search began immediately for someone or something to blame. There were many candidates. In a 1951 article for the *State* magazine, Bill Sharpe summarized: "The owners were charged with concealing defects in the ship, inspectors with collusion, the chartering company was accused of overloading her, the captain was accused of imprudent handling of his ship. The Life-Saving crew reached the wreck late, and then without sufficient equipment."

A thorough investigation concluded that no one could be held accountable. The biggest single reason that so many lives were lost was that, in the words of Dennis R. Means, "The station that could have best assisted the *Metropolis* had not yet been built."

In June 1878, in response to the *Huron* and *Metropolis* disasters, President Rutherford B. Hayes signed into law an act that increased funding for new lifesaving stations, expanded the active season to cover September 1 to May 1, and raised salaries to attract competent, experienced keepers. By the winter of 1878–79, North Carolina had eleven new stations.

These developments could not undo the tragedy of errors that sent the *Huron* and the *Metropolis* to their graves. However, there is some consolation in knowing that many similar tragedies have since been avoided.

CHAPTER 4

A Frightful Accident

THE WRECK AT BOSTIAN BRIDGE

– 1891 –

AS TRAIN NUMBER 9 RUMBLED THROUGH THE DARK
North Carolina countryside, fireman Warren Fry pulled the whistle
cord several times. The sound cut through the deep silence of the
August midnight like the cry of a lonely beast. A fourth-quarter moon

*The wreckage from train number 9 dammed up Third Creek, causing water to rise
in the second-class car. Passengers who had survived the crash were in danger of
drowning, and many did.* North Carolina Collection, University of North Carolina Library
at Chapel Hill/William Jasper Stimson

peered out from between the clouds, then vanished, then reappeared. Again Fry tugged the cord, warning all creatures great and small to clear the tracks.

Baggage master Hugh Leinster checked his watch—a large, lavishly engraved timepiece on a chain. Number 9 was running forty minutes late. At this rate, Leinster figured the train would arrive in Statesville at about 2:30 A.M.

Founded in 1789, Statesville was located in an area originally known as the Fourth Creek Settlement, an expanse of gently rolling hills in North Carolina's Piedmont section. The arrival of the Western North Carolina Railroad in 1858 had turned Statesville from a sleepy southern community (a visitor had once called it "as dull as hot, parching weather could make it") into a trading center of great importance. Proof could be seen in the August 20, 1891 issue of the *Landmark*, one of the city's two newspapers. Among ads for confectioneries and bakeries, clothing, furniture, and drug stores, the city's advantages were listed: three railways, a mean yearly temperature of 57.05 degrees, paved sidewalks and macadamized streets, a college, an electric light system, nine churches, three hotels, a national bank, a fire department, and numerous factories and businesses dealing in cotton, tobacco, flour, marble, herbs, and carpentry.

"It is a city of beautiful streets, handsome residences and business houses, refined and hospitable people and golden opportunities," the ad declared.

Hugh Leinster could vouch for the accolades bestowed upon Statesville. It was his hometown. At age twenty-four he was a well-known and popular young man, familiar with the generosity and kind-heartedness of Statesville's citizens. As he checked his watch in the early hours of August 27, 1891, he had no idea that the town's reputation for hospitality was about to be tested.

At 2:26 A.M. engineer William West—known as "Uncle Billy" to friends and family—pulled train number 9 into the Statesville station.

Uncle Billy was from Salisbury, 30 miles southeast of Statesville. Leinster knew the engineer and the town fairly well. The young baggage master's fiancée was, in the words of the *Landmark*, "a most estimable young lady of Salisbury."

In Statesville the train took on about ten passengers, including traveling salesmen Orville Lawson and George Bowley. Lawson sold millinery for a Louisville jobbing house; Bowley represented a rubber-goods company in Atlanta. They were headed for Newton, North Carolina, just 20 miles west of Statesville. Many years later Lawson still recalled the details of the trip: "That night we packed and prepared to get the train shortly after midnight. Turning our trunks over to Old Jerry [the porter], we left a call and went to our separate rooms for a few hours of sleep. Jerry called us promptly and we took that old horse drawn bus about 1 A.M. for the station about a half mile from the hotel." When the train arrived, they boarded the first-class car.

Fireman Fry pulled the whistle cord. Great clouds of steam spewed from the smokestack, and number 9 rolled out of the station, wheels clacking. As the coal fires burned hotter, it quickly picked up speed, settling into its familiar *chug-k-chug-k-chug* rhythm. The lights were low in the cars, and even passengers who were awake were tempted to close their eyes for a moment.

Shortly before 3 A.M., number 9 approached Bostian Bridge. The bridge, built in 1857, was a magnificent brick and granite structure with five arches that curved gracefully over Third Creek. Less than an hour earlier, another train had crossed Bostian Bridge safely. Number 9 would not be as fortunate.

In the first-class coach, conductor J. F. Spaugh took up the last ticket from the people who had boarded at Statesville. Passenger Marshall Nix dozed, enjoying the night air through a half-opened window. George Sanderlin, auditor for the State of North Carolina, was asleep in a bottom berth in the Pullman car. In the berth opposite him slept Col. Bennehan Cameron, a member of Governor

Thomas M. Holt's staff. Sanderlin and Cameron were headed for Shelby, where Sanderlin was scheduled to deliver a speech.

Suddenly the train made two jumps, then jerked forward and back. Sanderlin woke up. In the first-class car, conductor Spaugh reached for the danger cord. Before he could touch it, another jolt knocked him off his feet. Lawson, the millinery salesman, grabbed the seat in front of him. The train jolted and bumped, then plunged over the side of Bostian Bridge.

The distance from the top of the rail to the surface of the water was just over 60 feet. To the people onboard, the fall seemed to last an eternity. Col. H. C. Demming of Pennsylvania wondered why they were in the air so long. He tucked his pillow more securely under his head and reviewed his entire life, regretting that he had accomplished so little in the world. Auditor Sanderlin later recalled: "I felt myself going down, down, down. . . . I could [not] tell whither. My heart well nigh stopped beating."

As the train hit the ground, the sound of breaking glass and the hiss of escaping steam filled the night air. The first-class car landed on its right side, tilted at a forty-five-degree angle. Lawson landed on George Bowley, the rubber salesman. "That you, Louisville?" asked Bowley, who could not remember his new friend's name. "Yes," came the reply. "Is that you, Atlanta?"

The train's wheels continued to revolve noisily. Strong at first, the motor's pulse began to fade. Lawson and Bowley tried to get their bearings in the absolute darkness. All around them the cries and groans of the injured grew louder and louder. The two men climbed out a window. Lawson noticed blood flowing freely from several cuts, including a large one on the left side of his face.

The second-class car lay along the embankment atop the tender, a special car designed to carry fuel and water. Both were next to the engine, which had ploughed into the soft earth. The sleeper car lay with one end in Third Creek.

As the train hit the ground, the first-class car landed on its right side, tilted at a 45-degree angle. North Carolina Collection, University of North Carolina Library at Chapel Hill/William Jasper Stimson

Bennehan Cameron had been asleep until the moment of impact. Now he felt timbers closing in on him in his berth. He was certain he was doomed. Water began to rise to his chest, then to his neck. The wreckage had dammed up the creek. Cameron yelled for help. No one answered. He worked desperately to free himself.

Lawson and Bowley checked on fireman Fry and engineer West. Both were dead. The two salesmen scrambled the rest of the way up the embankment. Lawson later recalled that he pulled up briars and stickweeds that left permanent marks on his hands. The salesmen encountered conductor Spaugh with a lantern and followed him into town.

In Statesville a number of people had heard the crash but had not known what it was. They found out soon enough. Men dressed quickly and made their way to Third Creek by the half-light of the moon, which was still obscured from time to time by scattered clouds.

Colonel Cameron managed to free his left foot, which had been pinned by the wreckage. Trapped by the upper berth, he tried to lift it off its hinges. Finally he was able to raise the berth enough to come out from under it and crawl on top. He called for auditor Sanderlin but received no reply.

"Help!" cried a woman. "Please help! My daughter is dead and my leg is broken!"

Cameron found Mrs. W. E. Moore of Arkansas and got her out of the water. Her daughter, Ophelia, was not dead but had received a severe cut on her head.

Marshall Nix broke a window in the first-class coach and climbed out. He heard a splash and found another passenger floundering in the water. Nix pulled him out, and the two men decided to go into town for help. Lawson and Bowley had already reached the home of the railroad's section foreman. Lawson collapsed into a bed.

Back in the Pullman sleeper, auditor Sanderlin was emerging into consciousness. Staring upward through a window, he saw the moon. For a moment he could not imagine where he was. His gaze fell on the giant central arch of Bostian Bridge, and he began to realize what had happened. At the other end of the car, Louella Poole of Williamston, North Carolina, had managed to get an arm around her unconscious mother and was struggling to keep her from drowning.

"Is anyone there?" Miss Poole asked in a faint voice. "Can someone call for help?"

Sanderlin obliged, but to no avail. The situation grew worse by the minute. Tightly pinioned by timbers, Sanderlin could do nothing but shout for help. Exhausted and weakened by the ordeal, Miss

Poole finally had to let go of her mother. She had held on as long as she could. The water continued to rise, reaching Miss Poole's neck.

Colonel Cameron ensured the safety of Mrs. Moore and her daughter, then crawled back into the Pullman. He quickly regretted doing so. "The screams, groans and blood and the close atmosphere, together with the stun that I must have felt, together with the shock of the concussion, made me deathly sick," he recalled later. He raised a window on the top side of the car to get some fresh air. Somewhat revived, he called auditor Sanderlin's name again. This time, Sanderlin answered.

"I'm about to drown!" he exclaimed hoarsely.

Ignoring his own discomfort, Cameron plunged back into the death trap. He freed the auditor's body and raised the upper berth in order to help him out. "He was so heavy and so helpless that the weight of the upper berth which I was also holding was a terrible strain on my strength," Cameron said later. "But I managed to get him to the window." The colonel then turned his attention to Miss Poole. As he lifted her from the water, he felt someone else grasping at him.

Once Miss Poole was above water, Cameron grabbed the hands of another woman who was nearly submerged. He pulled, but her body did not move. A wire cord was stretched around her neck, and her gown was wound around the wire. Cameron winced as the wire cut into his hands, but he refused to give up. He later reported, "I got her loose and laid her upon a cushion and asked her name. She said she was from Memphis, but fainted before she gave her name." Cameron called out to see if anyone else needed help, but no one replied. He started for the embankment, then stopped to free a little boy from Reidsville, North Carolina, who had a bad cut on the side of his head. Cameron staggered up the hill, briars lacerating his feet like broken glass.

By then, survivors of the wreck were beginning to show up at various houses in Statesville. Colonel Demming, who had clambered out through an opening in the top and side of the sleeping car, made it to the residence of Gilbert Caldwell, about one-eighth of a mile east of the bridge. With Demming was Dr. Otto Ramsey, a passenger who happened to be a recent graduate of Johns Hopkins medical school. Eventually, Colonel Cameron also reached the Caldwell home. He rested for a brief moment and then, fortified by a glass of whiskey, asked to borrow the Caldwell's mule and buggy. Accompanied by Dr. Ramsey, he drove into town to alert as many people as he could and to send telegrams notifying the governor as well as friends and family of the victims.

Rescuers from town hastened to the creek. Statesville's many impressive amenities did not include a hospital, so the injured and dying were transported to the homes of such distinguished citizens as the Bostians, McRories, Andersons, Caldwells, and Bennetts. Several churches took people in, and Statesville's five physicians were pressed into service.

With daylight more townspeople appeared at the scene—some to help, others to observe. Railroad and government officials soon arrived. The editor of the *Landmark,* Joseph Caldwell, took notes for an issue of the newspaper that would be published later that same day. "A Frightful Accident," the headline would read. "A Passenger Train Jumps the Track on Bostian's Bridge This Morning—List of the Killed and Wounded—An Occurrence Without Parallel in the History of the State." The article noted that the entire train (engine, baggage and second-class car, the first-class coach, the Pullman sleeping car, and the private car of Superintendent Bridgers) had gone off the bridge.

"Some of the passengers had crawled from the car and were perched, dazed, on their tops," Caldwell wrote. "Axes were put to work and the cars cut open, and so many of the passengers as could be found were dragged out—some dead, some alive." In subsequent editions of the paper he provided additional details:

The high bridge apparently remained intact, but the rails were torn up and the edges of the stones were knocked off where the falling cars had come in contact with them. . . . Dead bodies were all about and the groans of the wounded saluted the ears of the workers. Willing hands, and not a few, were soon at work. . . . The dead were laid reverently on the ground. . . . While parts of the cars are in the water, the engine, looking like some great beast suddenly stricken helpless, lies on its side up and down the steep embankment.

The search for a cause began immediately. Some passengers claimed the train was traveling excessively fast; others said the speed seemed normal. A coroner's jury heard testimony from passengers, crew, and railroad officials. It reached the following conclusions:

- The train had wrecked because someone deliberately loosened a rail. (The railroad company was found negligent for leaving the necessary tools for such an act in an unlocked shed.)
- Cross ties at and near the break in the track were unsound and should have been replaced.

The jury also condemned the train's "high rate of speed."

In general, the public found these conclusions unsatisfactory. The Richmond & Danville Railroad insisted that it had only been a month since a work crew had checked and repaired the Bostian Bridge track. Attempts to find the person or persons who had tampered with the track yielded a number of questionable confessions, many by tramps who seemed primarily interested in free food and lodging at the local jail. No one was convicted.

Col. Bennehan Cameron was hailed as a hero. He, in turn, expressed appreciation to the people of Statesville: "No words could convey an adequate idea of the kindness of the people of Statesville and the railroad officials in ministering to the wants of the wounded and caring for the dead." He later sent money to Trinity Episcopal Church in Statesville for a memorial to those who lost their lives and as a reflection of gratitude to the town.

Of the fifty-two people on train number 9, twenty-two were killed and thirty were injured. Among the dead was young Hugh K. Leinster, baggage master. A trunk fell across him and although he was pulled from the wreckage alive, he did not survive. He was buried in Statesville on Friday afternoon, August 28. According to some reports, however, that was not the last time Leinster was seen.

Many years later, in the predawn hours of August 27, 1941, the Hayes family from Columbia, South Carolina, had a flat tire near Bostian Bridge. They did not have a jack with them, so Larry Hayes left his wife, Pat, and the children in the car while he walked to a country store a short distance away. As she waited, Pat heard the mournful whistle of a train in the distance. A light appeared, growing larger and larger. When the train reached the center of the bridge, the cars lurched and jumped the track. The sounds of breaking glass, shattering wood, and hissing steam followed.

Horrified, Pat rushed to the bank of Third Creek. She heard people screaming, saw them crawling out of openings in the broken cars. Suddenly there was someone beside her, and she nearly screamed in fright herself. The uniformed man's face was stark white. He held a large pocket watch in his hand. "Can you give me the time, Ma'am?" he asked. Pat told him, "Five minutes past three."

Before Pat could say anything else, the man's face seemed to fade, and she feared she was about to faint. A door slammed behind her. She turned and hurried to greet her husband, who had brought the store owner to help with the tire. Frantic, she insisted they come with her to the creek bank. When they looked down, there was nothing there.

Larry assured Pat that she must have fallen asleep and had a bad dream. Pat wanted to believe him, but the trainman with the watch had seemed so real. She talked Larry into stopping at the train station in Statesville the next day to ask about the wreck. An elderly man at the counter assured them that there had not been a wreck the night before. He then told them about train number 9 and the terrible disaster that befell its passengers and crew back in 1891. "In fact," he said, rummaging through some papers in a drawer, "It was exactly fifty years ago last night."

Since that time, people who love ghost stories have gathered at Bostian Bridge on numerous occasions, hoping for a glimpse of Hugh Leinster and his pocket watch. In August 1991, a century after the wreck occurred, a crowd of nearly 400 camped in a field just below the old bridge. Spectators came from as far away as Ohio. In an article for the August 27, 1991, *Statesville Record & Landmark,* Jimmy Tomlin described what happened: "The only headlights were those on the cars that began a steady exodus around 3:15. The only train whistles were cheap imitations made by human mouths."

Commented one observer: "I'm not surprised. Leinster's ghost found out what time it was from Pat Hayes back in 1941. He has no need to come back again."

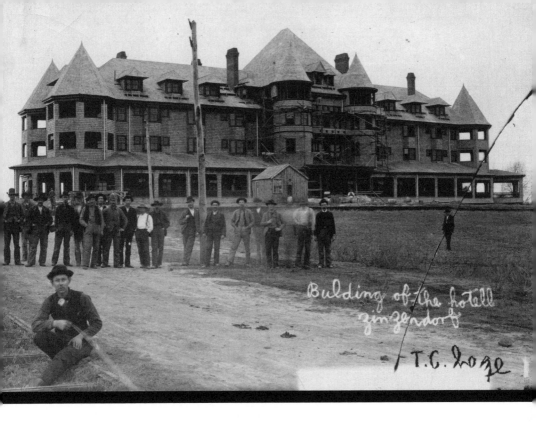

Bulding of the hotell zinzendorf

T.C. Loge

CHAPTER 5

Death of a Dream

THE HOTEL ZINZENDORF FIRE
– 1892 –

THE OFFER MUST HAVE BEEN HARD TO RESIST: "PURE,
bracing air, animating and cheerful surroundings, wholesome food
properly prepared and temptingly spread, and sweet downy beds that
lull to complete bodily rest." The ad that ran in May and June 1892 in
the *People's Press* of Salem, North Carolina, also promised "elevators,
electric lights, hot and cold public and private baths on every floor."
All this would cost the recipient "only what is reasonable."

The Hotel Zinzendorf under construction. Photo courtesy of Forsyth County Public
Library Photograph Collection

After reading the ad, even the residents of Salem and the neighboring town of Winston must have been tempted to pack a suitcase and hop on the electric streetcar that would deliver them right to the doors of the magnificent Hotel Zinzendorf. They might have imagined themselves in elegant evening clothes, waltzing to the music of a twelve-piece orchestra in the ballroom or strolling along the upper veranda, fanned by a breeze from the Blue Ridge Mountains, which rose like benevolent guardians in the distance. This hotel, the ad declared, was "the best ventilated, best drained and best arranged . . . in the South" as well as "the most convenient."

The Hotel Zinzendorf epitomized the carefree spirit of the early 1890s, a *joie de vivre* that later gave the decade its nickname the Gay Nineties. That spirit plummeted as early as 1893 with a financial panic and stock market crash, followed by depression and widespread unemployment. By then the hotel was gone, leaving behind fond memories of its brief reign as the crowning jewel in a glittering dream.

The dream began to take shape in 1890 when a group of businessmen saw potential in the undeveloped West End of the town of Winston. They knew that whatever benefited Winston would improve Salem, about a mile down the road. Winston and Salem were known as the Twin Cities or as Winston-Salem (although the towns would not officially be joined until 1913). Founded in 1849 as the county seat of Forsyth County, Winston was named for Major Joseph Winston, a Revolutionary War hero. Salem, incorporated in 1856, was originally laid out by Moravian colonists led by Count Nicolaus Ludwig von Zinzendorf. Its name was derived from the Hebrew word *shalom,* meaning "peace."

In 1890 prominent citizens of Winston-Salem included Richard Joshua (R. J. or "Dick") Reynolds, whose tobacco company was considered "*the* tobacco factory of the South." Wake Forest University and Salem College were well established as institutions of higher learning. The Twin Cities had macadamized streets, electric streetlights, railroad service, telephones, and electric streetcars. To the businessmen contemplating the potential of the West End, the time was right. When they were done, they decided, Winston-Salem would be known as one of the finest resort communities in the country.

Jacob Lott Ludlow, Winston's first city engineer, shared that vision. He designed dramatically curving streets, terraced lawns, and parks across the hilly terrain. The focal point would be a lavish hotel, built on a knoll at the head of Fourth Street (one of the highest elevations in Winston).

On October 9, 1890, the *People's Press* published a drawing of the Hotel Zinzendorf, "now under contract." The accompanying text said that the building "will be a beautiful large four story structure, with broken roofs, Queen Ann [*sic*] style, fitted and furnished in hard woods, with every accommodation that can add to the comfort of its guests." Named in honor of Count Zinzendorf, the majestic, 300-foot-long edifice was to have ten towers of various sizes and shapes. In addition to offering a panoramic view of the mountains, the Hotel Zinzendorf would overlook a huge forest where many of Winston-Salem's community leaders hunted wild game.

Even as the hotel's foundation was laid and each wooden beam put in place, Winston-Salem continued to grow and advance. Old Town (Trade) Street, the center of commerce in Winston, boasted a tobacco warehouse, two tobacco-manufacturing companies, two grocery stores, a boarding house, restaurant, saloon, dry-goods shop, farmers warehouse, and general merchandise store.

Salem's "Rough and Ready" fire company was justifiably proud of its steam pumper, which could throw water 135 feet—over the tower of Centenary Methodist Episcopal Church. The church itself was an object to be admired, with its seating capacity of 1,500, gas lighting, and central heating. Gothic arches, flying buttresses, stained-glass windows, and towers with ornamental woodwork brought it acclaim as "the handsomest and most attractive place of worship in the

State." Three small inns served the towns, but they would soon be eclipsed by the wondrous creation arising on Glade Street Hill.

By the time the ad for the Hotel Zinzendorf appeared in the *People's Press* in May 1892, yet another benefit had been added to the list. "Trotting over the hills . . . you come to the Marienbad and Mystic Parks springs. . . . Too great stress can not be laid on the mineral waters. They are most valuable, and are daily effecting remarkable cures. . . . On a single day not less than one hundred vehicles filled with people visited them to drink in new health."

Other ads on the same page of the newspaper touted "Lemon Elixir . . . for Biliousness, Constipation and Malaria" and "B.B.B.— Botanic Blood Balm," whose "almost supernatural healing properties" were "guaranteed to cure scrofula [a form of tuberculosis], ulcers, salt rheum [watery discharge from eyes or nose], eczema, and every form of malignant skin eruption."

Even with all its grandeur and grace, the Hotel Zinzendorf was not immune to criminal activity. In July 1892 the dead body of Ellen Smith was found in the woods behind the hotel. Her lover, Peter DeGraff, was arrested for the murder and executed in a public hanging. The incident inspired a song called "Poor Ellen Smith," recorded by The Kingston Trio seventy years later.

Overall, however, the hotel lived up to its image as a place where genteel folk could spend leisurely days, weeks, or months in the arms of luxury. With the completion of the Hotel Zinzendorf, Winston-Salem's hopes for success as a resort town seemed certain to come true.

In September 1892 Adlai Stevenson, Grover Cleveland's running mate on the Democratic presidential ticket, was an honored guest at the hotel. Newspapers all over the country reported the gift to Stevenson of "the left hind foot of a graveyard rabbit, a fetich [*sic*] which is said to invariably bring good luck to the possessor." As it turned out, Cleveland and Stevenson secured all eleven of North

Carolina's electoral votes and defeated Benjamin Harrison and White-law Reid in the national election.

Thanksgiving that year promised to be a gala affair at the Zinzendorf. A group of hunters, including Dick Reynolds, rose early and took to the woods behind the hotel with their shotguns. "It was a crisp autumn day with wind," one of the hunters recalled years later. "We got some wild turkeys and a large number of quail." The men brought the birds back to be cooked for dinner.

The aroma of freshly baked bread filled the hotel kitchen. With great care, cooks prepared vegetables and fruit from nearby farms. Milk was brought in from herds belonging to H. E. Fries, a local dairy farmer of great renown. The hotel's manager, E. S. Boswell, had worked in New York at the Manhattan Club. According to the Zinzendorf's ad, he had been commended far and wide for serving food "in the daintiest and most appetizing fashion."

Many of the guests made plans for a carriage ride later that day into Salem, where they would travel at a leisurely pace along elm-lined streets made of Belgian block. Others thought that perhaps it was a bit too windy for that. They planned to relax in their rooms, digesting what was certain to be a sumptuous Thanksgiving meal.

As 11:00 approached, everyone began to gather, anticipating the announcement, "Dinner is served." Instead, what they heard was a shout from the laundry room: "Fire! Fire!"

Flames shot out from the rear of the hotel. A call went out to fire companies in the area, prompting a race between two of them. Pulled by a team of powerful gray horses, one steam pumper reached Fourth and Liberty Streets in time to see the other one going down a hill. Its driver had freed his horses and hooked the steamer to an electric car. At the end of Fourth Street, about three-quarters of a mile away, a horrible cloud of dark smoke confirmed that a huge fire was in progress.

People at the scene of the blaze rushed through the halls, grabbing furniture and fixtures as they ran. Cadets from the nearby Davis

The Hotel Zinzendorf on fire, Thanksgiving Day 1892. Guests later shared what was left of a turkey dinner picnic-style on the grounds. Photo courtesy of Forsyth County Public Library Photograph Collection

School plunged into the burning building to rescue guests and possessions. A strong wind whipped the flames higher, helping them devour the hotel's wooden frame and cedar shingles. The *People's Press* later reported: "Coming down from the center of the roof, in the shape of a V, was the glowing, seething fire. Then, with wonderful rapidity, the flames sped on with wild, fantastic leaps, and ever increasing heat."

The driver of the horse-powered fire engine cracked his whip in the air. With a mighty burst of speed, his horses passed the electric car and arrived first at the Zinzendorf hydrant. A cheer went up from passengers and firemen alike. The *People's Press* later noted: "If this spirit animated everybody in Salem, we would startle the State."

Unfortunately, an enthusiastic spirit was not enough to quell the raging flames, nor was the Salem Fire Company's highly touted

"Rough and Ready" steam pumper. The pressure at the hotel hydrant was so low the water could not be thrown to any height.

"One miniature cyclone after another swirled out of the mass, with a diameter of about ten feet," recorded the *People's Press*, "hurtling viciously across the lawn, down towards the Salem line, sucking up burning cinders, ashes and dust and other debris, and carrying it skyward hundreds of feet." Large pieces of charred shingles were later found 4 and 5 miles away.

The heat was so intense, it cracked glass window panes in residences 2 blocks away. Homes and small farms between Fourth and Fifth Streets were in immediate danger of catching fire but were saved. For their owners, at least, Thanksgiving was a day for celebration.

People lingered on the grounds at a safe distance from the burning structure, personal possessions and hotel property piled around them. By 1 P.M. the grand hotel was in ruins. Onlookers and firemen joined in an impromptu "picnic on the grounds," sharing food that had been salvaged from the magnificent dinner-in-the-making. The feast did not include the turkey and quail bagged by local hunters. As Col. William A. Blair, one of the hunters, put it: "They were cooked all right, but never served."

The *People's Press* summarized the cause and effect of the destruction: "A building composed of most inflammable material, a gasolene [*sic*] stove, carelessness, no water, and there you go!" Although much of the loss was covered by insurance, no one stepped forward to rebuild the Hotel Zinzendorf in its original glory. Winston-Salem's dreams of becoming a famous resort town vanished.

Early in 1900 a commercial hotel called the Zinzendorf was built on North Main Street in Winston-Salem. It has since been torn down. Something of the flavor of the original Hotel Zinzendorf and the spirit of the Gay Nineties remains in the city's West End Historic District.

CHAPTER 6

A Wall of Water

THE SAN CIRIACO HURRICANE
– 1899 –

THE STORM HIT PUERTO RICO ON AUGUST 8, THE DAY the Catholic Church traditionally honors the martyr Saint Cyriacus. Puerto Ricans call him San Ciriaco, and in accordance with custom, that was the name they gave the cyclone that smashed into their island on August 8, 1899.

Winds reaching 100 miles per hour destroyed life and property, leaving thousands without shelter, food, or livelihood. On August 10, newspapers in the United States reported that 200 lives had been lost and the town of Ponce had been wrecked. The *Daily Republican* of Decatur, Illinois, included an ominous headline: "South Atlantic Coast Next . . . Warning Message Issued Today by the Weather Bureau."

Not much was left of the 643-ton barkentine Priscilla *when San Ciriaco finally departed on August 19, 1899.* North Carolina Collection, University of North Carolina Library at Chapel Hill/Charles Morgan

49

Eventually, the death toll in Puerto Rico would reach more than 3,000. Even as pleas for aid to the shattered island appeared in the American press, San Ciriaco blew through the Dominican Republic and brushed northern Cuba. On August 13 it passed the south Florida coast, just off Miami.

A day later the *Atlanta Constitution* declared that the storm was losing strength, adding: "Weather Bureau Hopeful. Hurricane Signals Hung at Atlantic Ports Have Been Taken Down and Vessels Have Been Notified That They Can Sail."

The hurricane was downgraded to a tropical storm on August 15. It bypassed Georgia and South Carolina, and the residents of North Carolina were cautiously optimistic. If the storm continued to curve northeast, the Tarheel State would also be spared.

San Ciriaco had other plans. It veered to the northwest, growing stronger again as it headed straight toward Cape Lookout.

A little bit further up the coast in Wit (later renamed Sea Level), John Styron had plans too. He and a group of about twenty other men were headed to Swan Island in Pamlico Sound for two weeks of fishing. This was no pleasure cruise. The men were after sea mullet, a popular inshore fish that was regularly shipped from North Carolina to distant ports. Styron and his friends rarely missed an opportunity to fish at this time of year. During these warm months you could wade into the surf and practically step on the mullet swimming around your feet.

The men knew there were storms in the area, but they could not let that stop them. They had families to support. Besides, a brisk wind would get the fish moving. Joining Styron on this mid-August "business trip" were relatives and neighbors who bore familiar Cartaret County names: Gaskill, Hamilton, Lewis, Rose, Willis, Salter, and Smith. As storm clouds gathered overhead, the men packed seven 20-foot skiffs (shallow, flat-bottom boats) with supplies. Included were homemade nets, an empty barrel, enough salt to cure a barrel of fish, and enough molasses, fatback, and corn for three days. Once that was gone, the men would live off the land and sea.

Styron and his comrades were all in their thirties and forties with the exception of fifteen-year-old William Henry Salter, who was filling in for his sick father. They were hardy and resourceful fellows, experienced in the ways of fish and the ocean. Their wives and children tried to keep that in mind on the blustery morning of August 16, 1899. They waved farewell as the skiffs headed up Core Sound.

By the time the fishermen reached Swan Island, it had begun to rain—hard. The group had no supper that night because conditions were too wet to build a fire. The rain continued. The next day the wind picked up steadily, growing louder and stronger, eventually reaching 100 miles per hour. The island was uninhabited and offered no shelter, so Styron and the others huddled under canvas sails in their skiffs while tides washed completely over the island. They bailed water as best they could, trying to keep the boats from filling. Soaked, chilled, and hungry, the men could only hope the weather would be better in the morning.

At daybreak on August 18, it appeared their wish had been granted. Everything seemed calm and peaceful on the island. Although the dark clouds on the horizon did not look friendly, the winds had subsided and the water had receded quite a bit. Exhausted from battling the storm, they debated what to do.

The mainland was less than 10 miles away, but it was likely to be a grueling 10 miles, considering that they could not put up sail. However, if they remained on Swan Island, they might starve. Most of the group decided to make a run for the mainland. Allen and Almon Hamilton declined, as did William and Washington Gaskill. They preferred to secure their skiffs and sit out whatever was left of the storm. They took down their masts and sails, threw their nets overboard, and hunkered down in their boats.

When Styron's group got about 3 miles from Swan Island, San Ciriaco returned in full force. The hurricane's eye had provided a lull, allowing the men enough time to leave but not enough time to get where they needed to go. Now they were at the mercy of fierce winds and frenzied waters.

Back on Swan Island the Gaskills and Hamiltons wondered if they had made the right choice. In later years "Wash" Gaskill often talked about his experience: "We knew the storm was a-comin' back," he would say in his distinct Outer Banks brogue. "And pretty soon she shifted to the nor'west and when we looked around we could see the Neuse River o'er the ma'sh [marsh] on Racoon Island. Looked like a wall o' water, 10 or 12 feet high a-comin' right down on us. Wurn't long a-fore it hit. We thought we were gonners."

When Gaskill was able to raise his head again, he saw parts of broken skiffs floating by on the choppy waves and a man clinging to an overturned boat. "Hit looked like young William Henry," he said later. "The last we seed o' him he was a-driftin' off t'wards Kinnikeet." The Gaskills and Hamiltons had made the right choice after all. They would survive the storm.

Meanwhile, the residents of Harkers Island were enduring their own version of San Ciriaco. Nearly 90 years later, Mary Willis could still recall every minute: "Yes heney, I 'member hit," she told author Sonny Williamson. "I'us about 14 I re'kon. It'us the worst time e'er been. I 'member the high toide busted the floor right outa Mama's ole house . . . Honey, we'us mommicked that day."

San Ciriaco "mommicked," or roughed up, a great many people that day. People on Hatteras Island watched in horror as water covered the entire island to a depth of 3 to 10 feet. They gathered together, forty or fifty in a house, only to be forced to abandon each refuge and head for another, wading through water up to their necks. Cattle, sheep, hogs, and chickens paddled or floundered helplessly.

Bellowing and squawking, they rolled their eyes in terror as they drowned right in front of their owners.

Out at sea John Styron and his fellow fishermen were not the only victims of the hurricane's lashing winds and mountainous waves. Seamen and passengers aboard numerous schooners and cargo ships also suffered the wrath of San Ciriaco. Fortunately for many of them, there were rescue stations all along the Outer Banks, thanks to the formation of the United States Lifesaving Service back in 1873.

Each rescue station was outfitted with lifeboats, life cars (watertight boats or boxes that could travel on a line from a wrecked vessel to the shore), and a two-wheeled cart containing such items as ropes, pulleys, cables, a small cannon for firing lines, and a breeches buoy, a life ring with canvas trouser legs.

At night surfmen patrolled the beaches carrying lanterns and signal flares. A flare could be sent up to warn ships away from the shoals, or to notify a boat in trouble that help was on the way. Patrols began at sunset and ended at sunrise.

The crew of the three-masted schooner *Minnie Bergen* was one of the many vessels that put Outer Banks lifesavers to the test during San Ciriaco's reign of terror. The 387-ton ship had been en route from Philadelphia to Cuba with a load of railroad iron, coal, and oil when it wrecked about a mile from the Chicamacomico Station. Rescuers set up their line-throwing gun, ran out the breeches buoy, and brought all seven crew members safely to shore.

At 3 A.M. on August 18, surfman Rasmus Midgett mounted his pony to begin his patrol for the Gull Shoal Station. Built in 1878, the station was about 12 miles south of New Inlet, which served as an entrance to the Cape Fear River.

Midgett came from a long line of seafaring men. His ancestor Abraham Midgett was a legend on the Outer Banks comparable to Paul Bunyon of the Northwoods. The first station keeper at Gull

Shoal had been Thomas P. Midgett, who was succeeded by Israel B. Midgett. At the time of San Ciriaco, the keeper was David M. Pugh.

As Rasmus Midgett headed out on patrol on August 18, he was already familiar with the destruction this hurricane was causing. Just two days earlier he had joined lifesavers from Chicamacomico and Little Kinnakeet stations in their attempt to rescue the crew of the schooner *Aaron Reppard*. Only three of the eight sailors had been saved.

Riding along the barren beach, past the remains of the *Aaron Reppard*, Midgett could almost hear the cries for help, the hoarse shouts of men who were about to die. He rode on for about half a mile, then stopped. The wind, though waning, was still strong. It could play tricks on a man's ears. Yet Midgett was almost certain he heard . . . Yes! There it was again!

The voices belonged to Captain Benjamin Springsteen and several of his crew aboard the 643-ton barkentine *Priscilla*. Springsteen had left Baltimore on August 12 for Rio de Janeiro. His ship carried freight valued at upwards of $34,000 as well as a much more valuable cargo: Springsteen's wife Virginia; the couple's sons, William and Elmer; and ten sailors. William served as mate, a position twelve-year-old Elmer hoped to hold one day.

The morning of August 18, even as John Styron and the other Cartaret County fishermen were debating over whether it was safe to leave Swan Island, the people on the *Priscilla* were wondering how they had survived the night. The wind had destroyed or blown away the vessel's riggings. Now the ship rolled and reeled as waves slammed the hull with relentless force. Springsteen wrapped his arms around his younger son, Elmer. His wife, Virginia, older son, William, and a young cabin boy named Fitzhugh Goldsborough clung to each other. Every time a breaker swooped across the deck, everyone shouted with terror.

All day the storm pounded the *Priscilla*. The wind howled and shrieked like a sea monster from an ancient myth. Then, at 9 P.M., the barentine struck bottom. Moments later a wave swelled to a massive size, towered over the boat, and descended with a roar. Springsteen felt Elmer being torn from his arms. He heard his wife scream. By the time he was able to open his eyes, Elmer, Virginia, William, and Fitzhugh were gone. Before Springsteen could even react to this tragedy, the ship's hull broke apart. He and the remaining sailors hung tightly to the wreckage, floating for hours until it, too, hit ground.

The men knew they must be close to shore, but they did not dare let go of the hulk that had saved their lives. The sea was still too angry. They were all weak; some were injured. With what little breath they had left, they called for help.

And Rasmus Midgett heard. He climbed off his pony and hurried to the edge of the seething ocean. About 100 yards away, he could make out part of a vessel with several persons hanging onto it. Now he had a decision to make. If he went back to Gull Shoals Station for assistance, it would take an hour to get there and another hour to return to the scene.

"Help!" yelled one of the victims. "She's breaking in pieces!"

Midgett's decision was made. He would do what he could do for them by himself. The waves continued to ebb and flow, and when they receded, he ran as close to the wreck as he could.

"Jump overboard—one at a time—when the water runs back!" he shouted to the stranded men.

Carefully timing his movements with the rhythm of the waves, he rushed into the surf when the water was lowest, calling out to each sailor in turn. He helped seven of the ten men to shore in this manner. Upon learning that the remaining three were too bruised and exhausted to make the leap, he swam out to the wreck. He carried them to shore one by one and placed them on a high dune where they

Rasmus Midgett's courageous rescue of the men from the Priscilla *during the San Ciriaco Hurricane was recreated in this painting by Hodges Soileau. The U.S. government awarded Midgett a gold medal of honor for his efforts.* Reproduction of painting courtesy of the U.S. Coast Guard

would be safe. A ragged piece of the wreckage had pierced Captain Springsteen's chest, and he was bleeding. Rasmus put his own coat around the injured man, then headed to the station for help.

Seven ships wrecked along the Outer Banks during San Ciriaco. Six others vanished at sea. The Diamond Shoals Lightship was driven ashore but was refloated and returned to duty.

The *Atlanta Constitution* reported the story under a series of grim headlines: "Terrible Record of Recent Storm." "Pamlico Region a Desert." "Full Number of Deaths Will Probably Never Be Known—Carolina Coast a Scene of Ruin."

The only survivors from the *Priscilla* were Captain Springsteen and nine sailors. Of the twenty men in John Styron's fishing party, only six survived. Drowned were Joseph and John Lewis; Henry and James Willis; Bart, William, John, and Joseph Salter; Micajah Rose; John, Kilby, Elijah, and Wallace Smith; and John Styron himself. The body of John Lewis was never found. Young William Salter's body was found several months later.

Stories of miraculous rescues and heroic efforts abounded. *The Landmark* of Statesville, North Carolina, printed a tale of two ships from Savannah en route to Philadelphia. Courtesy of San Ciriaco, they ran aground at Bogue Inlet. Stranded too far out for people on land to help them, they tied a line to an empty jug and cast it into the water. All night they watched and waited, willing the jug to reach the shore. It did. Lifesavers secured the line and the crews of both ships were saved.

On October 18, 1899, Rasmus Midgett was awarded a gold medal of honor by the United States secretary of the treasury for risking his own life to save the crew of the *Priscilla*.

One can almost imagine the original San Ciriaco, Saint Cyriacus, nodding with approval.

CHAPTER 7

Two Beasts in Deadly Combat

THE WILD WEST SHOW TRAIN WRECK

– *1901* –

THE COWBOYS CAME FIRST, WAVING THEIR BROAD-brimmed hats over their heads. Cantering on quick-footed quarter horses, they formed a tight circle in the middle of the large, open arena. Even before they finished, a band of German soldiers in chest armor galloped in on graceful white steeds. As they formed a separate circle, a blood-curdling yell announced the arrival of a band of Russian Cossacks in tall fur caps, waving long, curved swords as they urged

Crowds for Buffalo Bill's Wild West Show could always count on seeing exciting opening acts like the "Cavalry Maze," in which riders formed a circle in the midground, while others formed additional circles around them. Denver Public Library, Western History Collection, Nate Salsbury Collection, NS-268

their ponies forward. Colonial dragoons followed them, accompanied by Sioux warriors, South American gauchos, and Mexican vaqueros, shouting and firing pistols into the air.

As hooves thundered and dust flew, old men and women, young men and their "best girls," businessmen, parents, and children all rose to their feet with a cheer. They were no longer in Charlotte, North Carolina. They had been transported to a world more astonishing than any they had ever known. That was the magic of Buffalo Bill's Wild West Show.

William Frederick (Buffalo Bill) Cody had started the Wild West Show in 1883 and by 1901 it was famous throughout North America as well as abroad, where Cody was known as "Nature's Nobleman." In its heyday the show had 800 employees, 180 horses, 18 buffalo, 10 elk, 10 mules, 10 Texas steers, donkeys, and 2 bears. Among Cody's stars was a sure-shooting young lady, born Phoebe Ann Moses but known to audiences everywhere as Annie Oakley. Another featured performer was Johnny Baker, Cody's foster son.

In Charlotte the excitement began on October 27, when Cody and company arrived by train in two or three sections (accounts vary). They pitched their tents at Latta Park in Dilworth, a Charlotte suburb. Latta Park was the pride of Charlotte, featuring a lake, a lily-pad pond, a series of fountains, terraced flower gardens, and a network of meandering paths and drives. In the late 1890s, a bicycle racetrack, horse-racing course, football field, baseball diamond, and large grandstand had been added.

A *Charlotte News* reporter observed Colonel Cody's riders "at mess" in the park: "At one table are seated the Mexican vaqueros in their silver embroidered jackets and high comical hats. Then come the Cossacks in fur caps, the Boers in brown corduroys and big gray hats, the Baden-Powell men, the Canadian scouts, the cowboys, the life-saving crew and the Indians." (Sir Robert Baden-Powell was a famous British army officer.)

The reporter also inspected the riding stock, commenting that it mostly consisted of "sturdy little western range horses." However, there were some "noted specimens of equine beauty." One of these was Duke, an elegant chestnut stallion given to Cody by General Nelson (Bear Coat) Miles of the United States Army. Miles, an acclaimed soldier and Indian fighter, was a close friend of Cody's. According to Cody, Duke had exhibited before more people than any other horse alive.

Charlotte was the show's next-to-last stop of the 1901 season. Following an appearance in Danville, Virginia, the troupe would take a well-earned rest. As it turned out, that rest would begin sooner than planned, and under the most unfortunate circumstances.

On Sunday morning, October 28, crowds gathered to watch the parade march through Charlotte's principal streets, beginning and ending at the Boulevard. Not only was nearly every citizen of Charlotte in attendance, huge numbers of people had come to town from Gastonia, Concord, Monroe, Shelby, Lincolnton, Wadesboro, and other places. According to one estimate, the parade was seen "first and last, by over 30,000 persons."

Shows were scheduled for 2 and 8 P.M., with the price of admission set at 50 cents for adults and 25 cents for children under age ten. Reserved seats could be purchased for $1.00 at Jordan's Drug Store, at Tryon and Trade Streets. Transportation was no problem at all, thanks to an expanded trolley network with double tracks along South Boulevard and East Boulevard.

The show took place in an enormous rectangular tent. The *Charlotte Daily Observer* noted: "The management records that nearly 10,000 tickets were sold to the afternoon performance, the total number of spectators being, of course, in excess of this number."

After the band's rendition of "The Star-Spangled Banner," the audience was treated to the opening act—the Cavalry Maze—followed by a series of "historical" scenes, sharpshooting, racing, and rodeo-style events or, as one reporter put it, "a regular whirlwind of dare-devil riding, graceful manoeuvring [*sic*] and quick changing."

The Native Americans—all members of the Sioux nation—performed war dances and participated in dramatic reenactments of an attack on a wagon train and the capture of the Deadwood Stage, a mail coach pulled by six mules. Annie Oakley and Johnny Baker displayed their shooting skills. The U.S. Lifesaving Service gave an exhibition of their methods for rescuing people from shipwrecks.

Buffalo Bill received a standing ovation when he appeared on his spirited horse Duke. The *Charlotte Daily Observer* described Cody thusly: "He is a magnificent specimen of a man and carries lightly his 60 years. His hair is thinning and shows silver, but his figure is as erect as of yore and his eyes are still bright."

According to newspaper reports, a local man named Baby Ruth Craig called out an offer to buy Duke during the performance. Cody tried to ignore him, but Craig was not to be denied. He began to dicker with Buffalo Bill, raising his price to include the saddle and other trappings. Friends explained that the horse was a present from General Miles, and that Cody would hate to lose such a treasured gift. At last Craig understood. "He sat down again," the newspaper reported, "and made goo-goo eyes at an Indian chief, thinking the brave was a squaw."

Then came the grand finale: the "Capture of Pekin."

Back in August 1900, soldiers from eight nations had swarmed into Peking (Beijing), China, clashing violently with Chinese nationalist forces. The anti-foreign, anti-Christian "Boxers" (so called because of their expertise in the martial arts) were soon on the run.

An ad in the *Charlotte Observer* on October 27 and 28, 1901, described the reinactment of the battle as "a most exciting feature in which the Allied Powers of the world are correctly represented. The bright colored uniforms of the different forces make this one of the grandest spectacles ever witnessed."

The audience loved Buffalo Bill's "Battle of Tien-Tsin," politely overlooking the fact that the "Chinese soldiers" bore an uncanny resemblance to Native Americans. Cody's group of Sioux entertainers did triple duty in the show, portraying not only themselves but natives of Mongolia and China. This arrangement did not escape one keen-eyed newsman, who wrote: "Here the representatives from the armies of the powers fired upon, charged and finally captured . . . the Chinese, who were Mongolians after being Indians first, which socio-logical transformation is unique in history."

That night, tired but happy spectators made their way to homes and hotels, where they would dream of wild broncos and Arabian acrobats, the thundering hooves of a buffalo herd, clashing sabers, and the unearthly cry of the Cossacks. Children who had planned on dressing up as princesses or ghosts for Halloween now imagined new costumes, complete with feathers and fringe.

The stars of the Wild West Show headed for their "home away from home"—a train car. Their dreams would be of their real homes, the places that drew them like magnets at the end of each season. Those who had no permanent home weighed their options. A ranch in Arizona might need hands; a traveling circus might want to add an act. After the performance in Danville, Virginia, they would be free to go.

Before falling asleep, some of the performers may have thought back over the season, the highs and lows, the excitement and the occasional scare. They might have recalled what had happened that summer in a heavy fog a few miles east of Altoona. The locomotive of the show train's second section had crashed into the caboose of the first section. A tent man had been killed, six cars had been ruined, and four buffalo had escaped. The bison quartet galloped madly through the Pennsylvania countryside, alarming farm families, before finally conceding victory to a dozen Mexicans with lassos. The wreck had not been the first for the Wild West Show, but one could always hope that it would be the last.

It was after midnight in Charlotte when weary roustabouts finished loading horses, mules, steers, and buffalo into the extra-long stock cars. Cody checked on Duke and his other favorite horses: Old Pap, Old Eagle, and two stallions given to him by the queen of England. When he was certain that everything was under control, he retired to his private car, the last of twenty-one in the unit. The whistle blew, and the show train headed north into the cool, October darkness, gathering speed as it clicked along the rails.

The first unit of the show train pulled into Lexington, North Carolina, at about 3 A.M. The engineer saw a southbound freight train sitting on a sidetrack, waiting for him to pass. According to some accounts, he signaled the southbound engineer, a man named Lynch, to let him know there were more sections of the show train coming along. Other accounts state that engineer Lynch had already received orders from the Linwood station to wait for all sections of the show train to pass but misunderstood the orders. Some speculate that Lynch miscounted the number of sections that went by.

In any case, Lynch pulled his train onto the main line shortly after the first unit of the show train passed. He was rolling along a straightaway on a downgrade at 45 miles per hour when the glare of a headlamp emerged from a deep cut on a curve. Emergency brakes screeched. Sparks flashed as steel grated against iron. The trains began to slow down, but continued on their terrible course. When the engine crews had done all they could, they jumped off, hoping to save their lives. By then, both trains were traveling at about 8 miles per hour.

The predawn stillness was shattered by the sound of crunching metal and splintering wood. Annie Oakley was thrown from her berth and slammed against a trunk. Steam hissed from the crippled trains. The air was soon filled with the cries and groans of man and beast. Shaken and stunned, Buffalo Bill's employees quickly checked their own injuries. They were astonished and relieved to discover that none

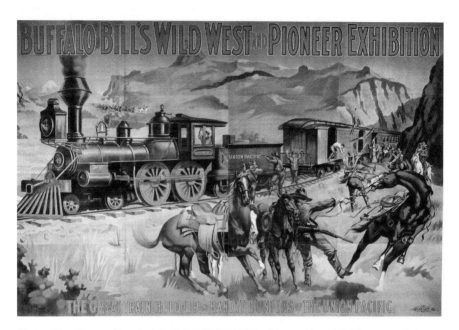

Posters like this one advertised Buffalo Bill's Wild West Show nationwide. The poster depicts a different kind of train disaster—a dramatic reenactment of a train robbery. Buffalo Bill Historical Center, Cody, Wyoming; 1.695.540

of them had been killed. Even those who had jumped from the moving engines had survived. The crew lit flares and went to investigate the damage.

Buffalo Bill bolted from his bed and rushed up the line toward the front of the train. What he saw shocked and sickened him. Horses lay everywhere, their bodies twisted into impossible positions. Mules rolled their eyes in terror and pain, struggling to lift legs that would never function again. The stock in the first five cars had been hit the hardest. In some cases, fragments of wood were driven through animals; one horse had been thrown atop the engine cab.

Cody felt as if he himself had been stabbed through the heart. The body on the engine belonged to Old Eagle, his star ring horse. He searched the mass of dead and dying creatures for Duke but did not see him. Nearby, Old Pap whinnied weakly and tried to raise his head.

"Get your guns," Cody barked to the crew. He blinked back tears forming in the corners of his eyes. "We'll do what we have to do."

Minnie and Belle Young, teenage girls who lived near Linwood, had come running when they heard the crash. They led a group of injured performers to their home. Mrs. Young immediately took on the role of chief nurse and cook, tearing up bedsheets to make bandages, and frying ham and eggs for the show people to eat. Returning from an early trip to the Old Red Mill, Mr. Young was surprised to find about 200 rough-looking visitors milling around his yard, many of them obviously foreign.

Down at the railroad tracks, the first rays of the morning sun revealed a hideous sight. Much of the wreckage was scattered down a 15-foot embankment, along with the mangled bodies of the horses and cattle who had been in the first five cars. Oscar Sisk of Salisbury, a retired railroad man, commented that the two engines seemed to have tried to devour each other. One had run halfway inside the other, and then they reared up on the tracks "like two beasts in deadly combat."

Cody had still not found Duke. The horse had been in the rear of one of the cars on which the engine's tender (a special car that carried fuel and water) now lay. Cody could not help wondering if the beautiful animal had been mangled beyond recognition. He was about to start going through the wreckage again when someone shouted: "Colonel Cody! Over here!" Through a nearby cornfield came one of the showmen, leading Duke. "I found him grazing out yonder," he said.

No one ever figured out how Duke ended up in the field, but the sight of him brought Buffalo Bill a note of cheer to counter the dirge that darkened October 29, 1901.

A total of ninety-two of the Wild West Show's horses died that day, and all six mules that pulled the Deadwood Stage were killed. The animals' bodies were sold to a Salisbury man for 50 cents each—the same price as an adult ticket to the show. Local veterinary surgeon Dr. D. H. Manogue examined and treated more than one hundred surviving horses. These were loaded on cattle cars and taken to the stockyards at Spencer, where they were cared for by Southern Railroad for a few days before being shipped to the show's winter quarters in Pennsylvania.

According to the *Charlotte Daily Observer,* "Engineer Lynch took to the woods shortly after the wreck, fearing violence at the hands of the showmen . . . and made his way to Holtsburg or some other place and getting away on the first train he could catch. Conductor Graves, of the freight train, resigned at once."

For a time, crowds flocked to the area where the wreck occurred in order to observe Native Americans and South American gauchos tending a small herd of buffalo not far from the tracks. The shaggy beasts had survived unscathed and proved a great curiosity until they, too, were shipped away.

In appreciation for help received from the Young family on that fateful day, Buffalo Bill gave Mr. Young a horse that had escaped injury. In 1974, at age ninety-six, Minnie Young Fitzgerald recalled that "Shoo-fly" was the fastest horse her father ever owned.

Cody's net loss from the wreck was estimated at between $40,000 and $50,000. His case against Southern Railway was finally settled over a year later. People wondered if the railroad would go bankrupt from paying the damages. Although the Wild West Show went back on the road, it never quite reached the spectacular level it had enjoyed before the North Carolina accident. Unwise investments contributed to its demise, and in 1913 the show was turned over to creditors.

The extent of Annie Oakley's injuries has been a matter for debate. One account states that she was partially paralyzed for two years. Another refers to "internal complications" resulting in hospitalization for several months. A torn kidney is recorded by yet another source. However, as biographer Shirl Kaspar points out, "An account in the *American Field*, written just one week after the wreck, said Annie received two slight injuries, one on the hand and one on the back." Kaspar adds that two months later, Oakley appeared in a shooting match in New Jersey, where she hit twenty-three of twenty-five live pigeons.

In later years Oakley claimed that her brown hair turned white seventeen hours after the accident. However, looking back, newspapers did not comment on this dramatic change in hair color until January 1902. It seems likely that someone would have noticed sooner. A reporter and friend of Oakley's suggested that a mishap in the baths of a health resort actually caused the sharpshooter's hair to turn white and that Oakley was too embarrassed to admit it. Annie Oakley never returned to the Wild West Show as an entertainer.

CHAPTER 8

Caught in the Middle

THE JULY FLOODS

— 1916 —

FOR SEVERAL WEEKS, COL. FRED OLDS OF RALEIGH
had been looking forward to traveling to the mountains. As far as
Olds was concerned, July was the perfect time of year to head for the
hills. His destination was Asheville, located in Buncombe County at
the junction of the French Broad and Swannanoa Rivers. The town

*During the floods of July 1916, fill material slid down a mountain near Old Fort,
leaving the track suspended.* Photo courtesy of the North Carolina Office of Archives and
History, Raleigh, North Carolina

was considered the cultural, resort, and economic center of western North Carolina.

Although the spring and early summer of 1916 had been dry in the Carolinas, a hurricane on the Gulf coast had recently brought relief. Rain was falling hard on July 14 when Olds arrived. The newspaperman, who was in his early sixties, had visited Asheville many times. On previous trips he had traversed the city on foot and by streetcar. He particularly enjoyed the attractions along the French Broad riverfront, which included a fine hotel, businesses, cafes, and street vendors. Riverside Park contained a zoo, Ferris wheel, movie screen, and baseball field.

A lifelong student and lover of North Carolina history, Olds also liked to stroll through Biltmore Village, a planned community created along the Swannanoa River in the late 1890s by philanthropist George W. Vanderbilt. The community housed nearly 300 people who worked at Vanderbilt's mansion and cared for the massive estate's gardens, parklands, and forests. With its English-style cottages and treelined streets, Biltmore Village reminded Olds of, in his words, "a little section of Coventry, one of the quaintest and most charming of all the old English towns."

As Olds entered his hotel on Friday, July 14, he was greeted by orchestra music. He recognized the song: "A Perfect Day" by Carrie Jacobs-Bond. With the rain pouring down, the day was not what Olds would have called "perfect." However, he could always hope tomorrow would be an improvement. He had no idea how far from perfect the next few days would turn out to be.

Conversing with the desk clerk, Olds learned that during heavy rains a few days earlier, the French Broad River had risen to nearly 9 feet—5 feet over flood stage. Fortunately, it was now receding. "I heard that a cyclone hit Charleston today," the clerk said. "I wouldn't want to live there."

Olds picked up a newspaper and went to his room to read the latest accounts of the fighting overseas. The British were reported to be holding their gains against the Germans near the Somme River in France. On the Eastern front a Russian advance along the Stokhod had been halted by Austrian and German forces. So far, the United States had remained neutral in the conflict, but tension between the United States and Germany was intensifying. That spring, Americans had been killed when a German submarine sunk the British steamer *Sussex*.

By Saturday morning, the level of the French Broad had declined to 4 feet. That same morning the center of the Charleston storm arrived in the mountains. Rain fell steadily all afternoon.

In Biltmore Village, Captain James Cornelius Lipe watched the weather from his home on the banks of the Swannanoa River. "The ground won't hold much more water," he commented to his wife, Sarah. "Maybe the rain will let up soon," she replied. Lipe hoped she was right, but just to be safe, he insisted that she take her mother and their crippled daughter, Nell, to stay with friends on higher ground.

In a house on Riverside Drive, Clara Belle Whitaker also listened to the pounding rain. She had lived along the French Broad River all of her eighteen years, dangling her feet in its cool depths on hot summer days, hunting tadpoles and salamanders with her younger siblings. As much as she loved the river, Clara knew that if it jumped its banks, she and her family could be in grave danger.

That Saturday, June 15, the weather station in neighboring Mitchell County recorded rainfall of 22 inches. Early Sunday morning, Asheville awoke to the clanging of the fire bell and the shrieking of the cotton mill's steam whistle. The rivers were rising.

In the predawn gloom Clara Whitaker's mother took the six younger Whitaker children to a friend's home on a nearby hill. Clara and her father stayed behind. They stacked many of their belongings on tabletops and carried others upstairs. It was not long before

In July 1916, flood waters swept buildings down the French Broad River, smashing them against railroad trestles and bridges like this one. "There goes everything we've worked for," said Clara Whitaker's father. It was the first time she had ever seen him cry. Photo courtesy of the North Carolina Office of Archives and History, Raleigh, North Carolina

Clara's father announced, "That's enough. We have to get out now."

"Let me get my pocketbook," Clara said. She ran upstairs, panic fluttering in her chest. Clutching what she thought was her wallet, she followed her father out of the house. They hurried across a wooden walkway he had built. Only after they reached dry land did Clara realize she was carrying a box of shoe polish instead of her billfold. It was too late to go back.

By 8 A.M. the French Broad was at 13.5 feet, nearly 10 feet above flood stage. Creeks, streams, and tributaries throughout the region were overflowing. At 9 A.M. the French Broad reached 18.6 feet. At 10 A.M. the bridge on which the gauge was located washed away.

Even as the bridge succumbed to the force of the flood, a group of one hundred volunteers assembled at City Hall to form the Citizens Relief committee. The sum of $2,300 was pledged on the spot. Clothing and bedding were promised. Shelter was offered to the homeless, whose numbers were expected to increase with each passing hour.

Colonel Olds, astonished by the news of the deluge, went to the Southern Railway bridge to get a good view of what was happening. He later described the sight that greeted him as "unreal," adding that "the Mississippi could have by no chance been muddier than that mountain river. And it roared and swirled and rose, not merely inch by inch, but foot by foot, and on its mad current came every kind of debris to be conceived of." He recalled that buildings floated by "as if guided by human hands, dwelling after dwelling, factory buildings one after another, each seeming to be sent down as a plaything."

One of the "playthings" taken by the river was Clara Belle Whitaker's home. She and her family watched, powerless, as the house bobbed along the flooded road, hit the train trestle, and burst into pieces. "There goes everything we've worked for," her father said. It was the first time Clara had ever seen him cry.

Olds made his way to the train station, where he discovered "two score engines . . . like terrapins, half out of the water, their shiny backs glistening near the round house." He later commented that the spaces between the passenger and freight cars looked like canals in Venice. Boxcars, oil tanks, and garages containing automobiles floated by. Olds commented that one massive building looked "for all the world like an ark. You almost looked for a giant steerman with his oar at the stern, guiding it through."

Like many areas, the Hans Rees Sons tannery district was swamped by the ever-widening French Broad River. The property included a group of houses where tannery workers lived. Men, women, and children marooned by the flood waved and shouted from the upper stories of rickety sheds.

Policeman Fred Jones noticed them early Sunday morning. He braved the tempestuous, rising waters in a small boat. When he arrived he was told that a man named G. W. Carson lay helpless in bed, ill with typhoid fever. Jones carried Carson to the boat, then rescued an infant and several women. By the time he got them to safety, the river had become too high and the current too strong for him to make another trip . Two firemen, Fred Gash and Everett Frady, soon appeared along with a number of other men who offered their assistance.

Local companies had hauled canoes and rowboats to the scene, but that solved only part of the dilemma faced by rescuers. At that point it would have been suicidal to set out across the raging river in a free-floating boat. Fortunately, there was another way. Firemen rigged up ropes and guides to enable safe passage. Everett Frady volunteered to go first. Hand over hand he worked his boat into the middle of the rushing stream. Suddenly the churning waters claimed his vessel, and he was left clinging to the rope for his life.

All over town, people found themselves suddenly standing on islands in the midst of a frothing, roaring stream. In Biltmore Village the quickly rising Swannanoa River caught Captain Lipe off-guard. He had thought he had time to secure his chickens and turkeys on the front porch. When he finished he waded through the flood waters with his seventeen-year-old daughter, Kathleen, another daughter, two nurses who boarded with the family, and the fifteen-year-old sister of one of the nurses. The captain intended to take them to the high ground beyond the Biltmore Estate's front gate.

"To my surprise," Kathleen later recalled, "as we crossed the train tracks, the water became deeper, the current more swift. By the time we reached Lodge Street, the water was almost over our heads. Torrents from broken dams upriver had changed the course of the Swannanoa. We were caught in the middle of a wide, wild river."

Back at the French Broad, fireman Frady worked his way along the rope the rest of the way to the tannery. Fireman Fred Gash then attempted to take a boat across. He succeeded. Other rescuers soon joined in, and thirty-five men, women, and children were taken out safely. Before anyone could breathe a sigh of relief, shouts were heard from a brick building on the far side of the tannery grounds. People appeared in the upper windows, calling for help. The crowd onshore could see that one of the women was holding a baby.

Once again Frady and Gash braved the boiling river. As onlookers watched, enthralled, the two men constructed a walkway between the building where the victims were stranded and a building closer to the spot where they had fastened their boat. They helped several people out onto the roof, one by one. Reassured by Frady's calm confidence, the woman with the baby handed him her child. Soaked and shivering, the group proceeded gingerly over the walkway, well aware that they might slip and fall into the forceful current at any moment. A cheer went up when the entire party arrived safely onshore.

Kathleen Lipe's group did not fare as well. Although they all managed to grab onto a tree outside the entrance to the Biltmore Estate, attempts to rescue them by canoe and horseback failed. A lifeguard tried to save Marion, the fifteen-year-old girl, but she panicked and fought against him. The lifeguard could not hold onto her and she went under. Her sister Charlotte became hysterical. Minutes later, she released her hold on the tree and disappeared.

Some time after that, Captain Lipe also let go of the tree. Kathleen thought perhaps he had a cramp. He reached for another tree but missed it and was swept away. Kathleen closed her eyes and prayed for the strength to hang on. When she opened her eyes, she was alone. Vickie, the other nurse who had boarded with the Lipe family, had vanished without a sound. Feeling weaker by the minute, Kathleen continued to pray and to hope her father and the others would be saved. She knew they were not only in danger of drowning but of being struck by huge chunks of debris carried by the swollen waterways.

Observing Biltmore Village from the Asheville side of the Swannanoa, Fred Olds noted with dismay, "The houses were only half out of the water. One would never by any chance, if he had just come from Mars, let us say, have known that there was a railroad, a street car track, and a bridge and people living there."

Finally, Kathleen Lipe saw a lifeguard swimming toward her. He tied her securely to the tree. At that moment, she said later, she knew she would survive. That afternoon, eight or nine hours after she had left home to seek higher ground, two men lifted her into a flat-bottomed boat and took her to a hospital. Her home stood until the water subsided, then collapsed into the Swannanoa.

Fred Olds returned to his hotel, overwhelmed by the "awful, gripping terror" of the flood. The next morning, the *Asheville Citizen* announced: "Asheville today is absolutely isolated from the outside world, is a city of darkness void of ordinary transportation facilities, and finds herself helpless in the grasp of the most terrific flood conditions ever known here."

"The damage at Biltmore is frightful," the newspaper declared on July 19. "All hydraulic plants located on the French Broad river are under water and it probably will be days before gas or electric power can be generated." Hundreds of people wandered around town, dazed and hungry.

Kathleen Lipe and most of her family survived. Her father did not. The two nurses—Charlotte and Vickie—and Charlotte's sister Marion also perished. In the days that followed, reports of destruction and devastation surfaced throughout the region, as did stories of heroism and sacrifice.

"Asheville rose to the heights of the occasion," Olds declared, "just as the river had risen; matched her courage and with pocketbook, too, everything the cruel and crafty river had done."

The flood of 1916 was blamed for eighty deaths in Alabama, Mississippi, Tennessee, and the Carolinas. Property damage was estimated at $22 million. The Southern Railway suffered the greatest single loss of property, yet within ten days limited rail travel was restored.

Col. Fred Olds died in 1935 at age eighty-two, having devoted his life to preserving and sharing the history of North Carolina. "He knew every hog path and bypath of the state's 100 counties," noted the *Charlotte Observer*. The North Carolina Museum of History owes its existence to his dedication and passion. A statue honoring him stands at the museum entrance.

Kathleen Lipe eventually became a teacher, wife, and mother known for her intelligence, optimism, and generosity. She died in 1989 at age ninety. The tree that saved Kathleen's life survived. Writer Lyn Leslie described it in 2003: "A maple . . . still as strong and healthy as it was on that summer day so many years ago . . . quietly stands guard in its position, third on the right from the lodge gate."

July 1916 was not the first time the mountains of western North Carolina were subjected to flooding, nor was it the last. Floods swept through the area in 1940, 1964, three times during the 1970s, and four times during the 1990s.

In May 2004 the *Asheville Citizen-Times* published an interview with Clara Belle Whitaker Edmonds, who was celebrating her 106th birthday. She remembered the 1916 flood clearly, describing how, in her panic, she saved a box of shoe polish instead of her pocketbook.

Four months after the interview, a series of hurricanes along the east coast delivered torrential rains to Asheville and surrounding areas. Over a two-week period in September, the remnants of Hurricanes Frances and Ivan besieged mountain communities with high winds and flooding, followed by additional rain courtesy of Hurricane Jeanne. Clara Edmonds passed away during Ivan. Her death was not connected to the storm, but her granddaughter's house was washed away, just as Clara's had been in 1916.

The Biltmore Estate, which lost its nursery during the 1916 flood, survived the 2004 floods without damage. At the writing of this book, Kathleen Lipe's tree remains on guard at the entrance.

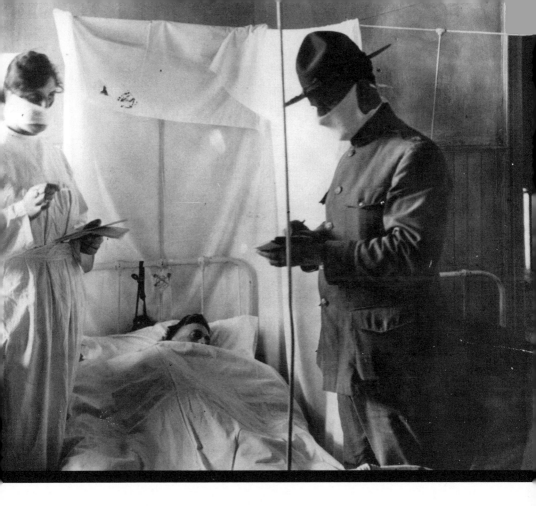

CHAPTER 9

Killer on the Loose

THE INFLUENZA PANDEMIC

— 1918 —

IN THE FALL OF 1918 A KILLER ARRIVED IN NORTH Carolina. There was no WANTED poster in the post office and no blockade at the border. The killer entered the state as freely as a September breeze. A murder spree was in the making—and no one was safe.

During the influenza pandemic of 1918, the American Red Cross distributed posters like this one nationwide to underscore the seriousness of the outbreak and to illustrate the use of protective masks. Courtesy of the American Red Cross Museum. All rights reserved in all countries.

79

Mary Lee Rankin was twenty-four, a science teacher beloved by her students. But by 2:30 on the afternoon of October 4, she was dead.

Two-year-old Georgie Mason was his parents' pride and joy, but the killer did not care. Georgie died on October 6. The next day the murderer returned for Georgie's mother.

Dorothy Crosby was only five; her sister, Mary Elizabeth, ten. They were buried in a double funeral on October 9.

Albert Waltman, age thirty-two, had a promising career with the telephone company. Waltman's wife watched him die on October 11, and his two daughters were left fatherless.

Like many criminals, the murderer had several aliases: the blue death, the Grippe, the Spanish Lady. Unlike most criminals, this one could not be put on trial or locked behind bars. The police had no authority or power. Instead, doctors and nurses found themselves trying to arrest one of the deadliest enemies they had ever encountered: influenza, also known as "the flu."

There had been warnings. Back in March, influenza had struck in several states, most notably in army camps, leading to many deaths. However, life-threatening disorders and epidemics were common in 1918, particularly in military camps. Yellow fever, smallpox, rabies, diphtheria, typhoid fever, and meningitis struck repeatedly. State and local health agencies were not in regular contact with each other, and the number of influenza deaths had not raised any alarms.

People who suffered from the flu in the spring of 1918 had the usual symptoms—body aches, muscle and joint pain, headache, sore throat, unproductive cough, fever, and nausea. In addition, this version of the grippe had its own peculiarities: Deaths seemed to be concentrated among people between ages twenty and thirty instead of in the customary group, the very young and very old. Doctors also observed that individuals who died from the flu or subsequent pneumonia that spring suffered bleeding and swelling in the lungs not normally associated with influenza.

These unusual features were duly noted, but not deemed significant. There were so many other things going on in the spring of 1918. Foremost on everyone's mind was the war. Sparked in 1914 by the assassination of Austrian Archduke Ferdinand, the conflict pitted the Allies (mainly France, Great Britain, Russia, Italy, Japan, and the United States) against the Central Powers (mainly Germany, Austria-Hungary, and Turkey).

American troops were being shipped overseas by the thousands: 84,000 in March and 118,000 in April. They carried machine guns, rifles, pistols, and plenty of ammunition—none of which would prove as deadly as the virus they unwittingly transported within their bodies.

In late spring and summer 1918, influenza killed hundreds of thousands of people in Europe, the Middle East, and Asia. Governments involved in the war censored reports concerning the huge number of flu-related deaths in their countries to avoid revealing weaknesses to the enemy. Spain, however, was not a participant in the war and had no reason to conceal its health problems from the world. When an estimated eight million of its citizens succumbed to the flu, Spanish newspapers reported the outbreak on their front pages.

Unaware of the origin or extent of the scourge, everyone outside Spain began calling it "Spanish influenza." The Spanish, on the other hand, referred to the disease as "the French flu." They claimed it had come from the battlefields of France.

As the transfer of American soldiers to Europe continued—279,000 in June, over 300,000 in July—the virus mutated, increasing its potency against otherwise healthy individuals. At the end of August, it returned to American shores. More than one hundred sailors at Commonwealth Pier in Boston reported to sick bay.

Even then, the country was still more engrossed in other news items of the day, including the women's suffrage movement, the espionage trial of socialist Eugene V. Debs, and the Bolshevik uprising in Russia. It was not until September that America realized this was not

THE WAY THE GERMANS DID IT AT CHATEAU-THIERRY

THE WAY NORTH CAROLINIANS DO IT AT HOME

The North Carolina State Board of Health emphasized that failure to take precautions against influenza could cause death just as surely as bullets fired by enemy soldiers in battle. Illustrations are from the October 1919 Bulletin of the North Carolina State Board of Health, courtesy of the State Library of North Carolina.

just another round of the flu. Victor Vaughn, the surgeon general of the army, reported from Camp Devens near Boston: "I saw hundreds of young stalwart men in uniform coming into the wards of the hospital. Every bed was full, yet others crowded in. The faces wore a bluish cast; a cough brought up the blood-stained sputum. In the morning, the dead bodies are stacked about the morgue like cordwood."

This version of influenza seemed to develop into pneumonia just when victims thought they were getting well. As their lungs filled with bloody fluid, their skin usually turned a dark bluish color. The disease acquired a new nickname: "the blue death." Massachusetts announced that an epidemic was under way. The United States surgeon general—named, ironically, Rupert Blue—ordered the printing and distribution of health alerts and provided key information to newspapers on how to recognize and treat influenza.

Port cities along the East Coast felt the effects first as military ships carrying doughboys home from Europe docked and their passengers disembarked. Among these unfortunate coastal towns was Wilmington, North Carolina. Under the headline "Epidemic of Influenza Spreads to 36 States," the *Charlotte Observer* of October 1, 1918, commented that Wilmington had been "hard hit." A separate article declared: "In her valiant struggle with the epidemic of Spanish influenza, which apparently has reached the proportions of a scourge, Wilmington has the sympathy of the whole State."

The same edition of the *Charlotte Observer* warned: "Advance Guard of Grip is Here. Health Department Prepares for Great, Rapid Spread. Three Cases of Spanish Influenza Reported to Dr. Hudson with Four Suspected Cases." (Dr. C. C. Hudson was the city health officer.) Charlotteans feared the numbers could only go up. They were right. Camp Greene was located just northwest of town, and influenza thrived at military bases.

Named for Nathanael Greene of Revolutionary War fame, Camp Greene was a massive facility containing approximately 2,000 buildings on 2,340 acres of land. It was a relative newcomer to Charlotte, having opened at the end of August 1917.

In the fall of 1918, Joseph B. Mathews, a private from Massachusetts, was working in Camp Greene's base hospital. On September 24 he wrote to his girlfriend: "I just heard now that there are half a dozen cases of that Span[ish] Inf[luenza] here. Its bad stuff according to Northern papers. My sister Mary had it. Last accounts she was nearly well but I have not heard for a few days."

At first, officials denied any plans to quarantine the camp because of the flu. Then, the number of cases known to exist in Charlotte suddenly leaped from 3 to "in excess of 40." On October 3 the *Charlotte Observer* reported 100 cases and one death from influenza. In one elementary school, three-quarters of the children were suffering from the disease.

Dr. Hudson issued recommendations for treatment: "Go to bed. Take a purgative medicine. Follow this in a few minutes with proper doses of quinine and aspirin, which may be repeated every two or three hours until several doses have been taken. Call a physician, but do not delay your own treatment until his arrival, as all physicians will be very busy. . . . Attendants upon those having this disease should wear a strip of cloth across nose and mouth which is moist with a germicide."

Matters were soon complicated further by a shortage of physicians and nurses, partly because so many of them had been called into service in Europe and partly because they were not immune to the flu themselves.

The number of people with the flu at Camp Greene reached 204 on October 3. Although the cases were reported to be of the "mild type," the camp was quarantined against all visitors. The commander announced that the order would probably be in effect for about ten days.

By then the disease had gained considerable ground in the state. Reports from Raleigh on October 4 revealed that more than 8,000 cases had been recorded in North Carolina "to date" (Wilmington accounted for 6,000) and that more than fifty deaths had resulted from pneumonia following the flu. One of these was Mary Lee Rankin of Charlotte, who had recently turned twenty-four.

On October 5 officials quarantined the city of Charlotte: "Schools, Churches and Theaters Closed and All Public Indoor Meetings Forbidden Until After October 15," the announcement read. "Drastic Action Intended to Prevent Conditions Getting Beyond Ability of Doctors and Nurses to Attend Sick—Nearly 200 New Cases Raises Reported Total to 400."

Private Mathews of Massachusetts wrote about the situation at Camp Greene: "The old flue is raising cain. . . . Our service has had the eight wards on D row with mine as headquarters. . . . I have flu wards on all sides of me. . . . There was several records broke in regards to number admitted & all kinds of work. . . . Very industrious bunch, most all wearing gauze masks. The old ambulances keep up a steady stream, 8 or 10 patients in each load. . . ."

A pall fell over the city. In the words of one reporter, the streets took on a "sabbath appearance." The quarantine order, signed by Mayor Frank R. McNinch, specified that no one who had the flu could leave his house until "after the seventh day from day of onset of the disease." A child living in a house where influenza existed could not leave the premises until "after the twelfth day from the day of onset of the last case of this disease."

It was unlawful to "conduct, keep open, or enter for the purpose of patronizing or loitering, any vaudeville or moving picture or other theater, billiard or pool room, bowling alley, shooting gallery, dance hall or other public places of amusement or resort . . . to hold any meeting or gathering in any church, Sunday school, lodge or society hall . . . or to keep open any public or private school." Violation of the law would result in a $50 fine (comparable to about $600 today).

The American Red Cross mobilized its forces, enrolling nurses and providing hospital supplies in cooperation with the public health service and state boards of health. Department heads of the Charlotte chapter developed a plan to ascertain hospital facilities (number of beds and space for extra beds), number of graduate nurses available, and type and quantity of materials and supplies accessible in Red Cross work rooms. The chapter also enlisted and organized volunteers to perform a wide range of services. A canteen was established to provide meals for homes where all members of a family were sick.

Every day notices of illness and death filled the newspapers as communities across the state were put under quarantine. Forty years later, Katherine McKinnon, a nurse in training at Charlotte's Presbyterian Hospital at the time, still vividly recalled conditions there:

> Everywhere [in the hospital] was filled. The halls, the parlors. Any available space where you could put a cot for someone to be on . . . I remember a little blonde girl with the prettiest blue eyes. She was about four years old. Looked like a wax figure. She was the sweetest thing. It just killed me when she died. I just thought I couldn't live. It still hurts. There wasn't even a room for her. She was in a little crib out in the hall.

The number of deaths at Camp Greene grew so high that undertakers were overwhelmed. Funeral processions down Trade Street were a daily event; coffins were stacked like firewood at the Southern Railway Station, waiting for trains to take the bodies home.

On Wednesday, October 9, the *Charlotte Observer* shared what appeared to be good news: "Hudson Thinks Epidemic Here May Be At Crest." Yet a subheading acknowledged 130 new cases of the blue death. Another page of the same issue covered the deaths of two-year-old George W. Mason Jr. and his mother, Pearl. Mr. Mason, the newspaper reported, "is seriously ill at his home with the same disease." Directly below that article was a paragraph about William Alonzo Harkey, age sixteen, who had died following "an attack of pneumonia super-induced by Spanish influenza."

An announcement of the Crosby sisters' double funeral appeared the next day (Thursday). "The deceased are survived by the parents and three sisters," the newspaper reported, adding, "Another child is seriously ill with the same malady." Another article covered the death of three-year-old Ruth Ingle, whose father was serving with the American army in France. Albert Waltman's death notice appeared on Friday.

Even as influenza was described as "decreasing" in the eastern part of the state, Charlotte's mayor decided to extend the quarantine for another week. That same day, Charlotte Caldwell McCullough responded to a call for help from a friend. She found the woman, her two little sons, two acquaintances from Greensboro, and the maid all suffering from influenza. They had been under a nurse's care, but she had become ill and had been taken to the hospital. Mrs. McCullough and several other friends of the sick woman agreed to take over the care and comfort of the six ailing people.

The grippe continued to spread. According to the war department, more than 3,000 cases had been reported at Camp Greene since September 13. Pneumonia cases totaled 308. The number of deaths was 93.

Day after day, the *Charlotte Observer*'s "Society News" presented information about flu victims. Included in one issue was Charlotte Caldwell McCollough. Five days after arriving at her sick friend's apartment, she succumbed to the flu herself. She died two days after that. Named for the city of Charlotte, Mrs. McCullough was seen as an example of the willingness to sacrifice exhibited by so many of the town's citizens during the epidemic. As Dr. Charles M. Strong put it, "There was no panic, hysteria, and few tears, but, instead, a calm, unselfish devotion to duty."

At the same time, America's armed forces were demonstrating those traits on foreign battlefields. In mid-October President Woodrow Wilson rejected a German peace proposal that fell far short of terms the Allies were willing to accept. The war against the Central Powers was not over yet.

Nor was the war against the blue death. In the words of Dr. Charles M. Strong, "Its advance was like the first advance of the Teutonic Horde—marched steadily forward until it captured its every objective."

On October 19 the *Charlotte Observer* reported that officials of Mecklenburg County and the City of Charlotte had extended the quarantine for another week. October 20 brought news of worsening conditions. The eastern section of the state requested ten emergency nurses from Charlotte. "The request could not be granted," said the newspaper, "as every available nurse in Charlotte is at present employed either in this city or as a volunteer in nearby cities."

The University of North Carolina at Chapel Hill prepared to lift its quarantine, announcing that although an estimated 300 students had been stricken, only three deaths had occurred as a result of the disease. That number increased on October 26. At age forty-two, Dr. Edward Kidder Graham, president of the university, died of pneumonia following influenza. He had been sick less than a week.

Although the Charlotte quarantine was extended once again on November 1, conditions were definitely improving by then. The Charlotte chapter of the Red Cross closed the canteen it had been operating. The quarantine was lifted on November 7. Official records at Dr. Hudson's office showed that influenza and pneumonia caused 111 deaths during the epidemic. The number of cases had probably reached 5,000. Compared to many other places, Charlotte's casualties were light. Philadelphia was the hardest hit of all American cities, recording more than 12,000 deaths.

On November 11 Charlotte joined cities all over the world in celebrating the armistice that officially brought World War I to an end. "Had quite a parade and fireworks and every auto had a tinware store tied on to it," Private Mathews wrote from Camp Greene. "Then at nine thirty they had a dance on the a[s]phalt pavement on Trade street and quite a time was had by all."

Camp Greene closed quickly once the war was over. The City of Charlotte dedicated a section of Elmwood Cemetery to those soldiers who died at Camp Greene but whose bodies had never been claimed.

In spite of the destruction the influenza epidemic caused, in North Carolina, as in many other states, there was also a lasting positive result. Medical facilities were upgraded immediately. New hospitals were built. According to one physician, the early 1920s witnessed the "greatest hospital movement" in North Carolina's history. Public health institutions across the state received more attention and more funding. New county health departments were established.

The influenza pandemic of 1918 cast a very long shadow over North Carolina, the United States, and nearly every country on earth. It was neither the first major outbreak of the disease nor the last. The flu continues to be a source of concern worldwide, and research is ongoing.

CHAPTER 10

No Use Being Sorrowful
THE COAL GLEN
MINING DISASTER
— 1925 —

JOE HUDSON'S WORKDAY BEGAN WITH A RIDE IN A
car—not a Model T or Dusenburg, both of which were popular in
1925, but a small, open car that resembled a wagon. On his cap he
wore a light powered by a battery strapped to his back. He rode the
car downhill on a track into a deep, dark underground passageway—
1,000 feet, 2,000 feet. Safety lamps burned here and there in the cav-
ern, offering small comfort in a world of stone-cold blackness.

As a crowd gathered to see what was happening at the mine, workers erected a
"corral" of ropes and wires to prevent onlookers from getting too close. North
Carolina Collection, University of North Carolina Library at Chapel Hill/Ben Dixon McNeill

Hudson, age twenty-seven, worked in the Coal Glen mine. Created by the Carolina Coal Company in 1921, the mine was located on the Deep River in Chatham County, North Carolina. Coal Glen mine employed about one hundred miners, timbermen, trackmen, chainers, hoist operators, machine operators, and hoisting engineers. Inspired by the success of mining in Alabama, the Carolina Coal Company had visions of Coal Glen becoming a "future Birmingham."

It was a tough way to earn a living. As local resident Jeter Adcock later recalled: "In those days men worked eight and ten hours. There weren't any cigarette breaks or coffee breaks or Coca Cola breaks. When you finished a day in the mine, you were ready to sit down for awhile."

Mining was often a family affair, and that was true for Joe Hudson. His sixteen-year-old brother, Dan, worked as a track helper. Another brother, J. M., was a miner. Their brother-in-law, Sam Napier, was a machine helper. Employees at Coal Glen mine came from several states, including West Virginia and Alabama, and from the neighboring counties of Lee, Randolph, and Moore in North Carolina. They lived with their families in the village of Coal Glen, where identical houses stood side by side. They shopped at the company store, buying goods "on account." A baseball field offered opportunities for recreation.

Coal Glen was in North Carolina's Piedmont section, a region of flat-topped, sandy ridges and broad, flat valleys. Forests of longleaf pine, hickory, and red maple brought rich color to every season. In the spring and summer, wildflowers brightened the woods and fields. Sparrows, warblers, and tanagers chirped friendly greetings from the trees.

The men who worked in the mines did not have much of a chance to savor this natural beauty. The songbirds they were most familiar with were the canaries brought underground to serve as an early-warning system. Canaries usually chirped constantly. If one stopped singing or was found dead, miners got out as quickly as possible to escape the toxic gases that had affected the bird. Mixtures of gases, known as "damps," were a particular hazard. Following an explosion, an "afterdamp" (mostly carbon dioxide and nitrogen) was almost certain to kill anyone who survived the blast.

The Deep River coal mines were unusually prone to the formation of methane, which became explosive when mixed with air. This fact had been discovered long before the Carolina Coal Company embarked on its mission. Around the turn of the century, following two explosions in which more than seventy miners were killed, the Egypt Mine on the other side of the river from Coal Glen went bankrupt. It reopened in 1915 under the ownership of Norfolk-Southern Railroad. Renamed Cumnock, it had supplied coal exclusively to the railroad for a time.

By spring 1925 Carolina Coal was showing a profit. Erskine Ramsay Coal Company had taken over the Cumnock Mine. Both had installed new and improved machinery, and the future looked bright.

On May 27 Joe Hudson was on day shift. He reported to the mine at 7 A.M. The air was chilly. Temperatures had been unseasonably cold, dipping into the low forties overnight. There was a cotton field near the mine-owned houses, and someone had recently remarked that the crop looked like "a cake of soap after a hard day's washing."

That morning a couple of day-shift employees failed to show up for work. One of them was sleeping off the effects of a drinking binge. Even though manufacturing, selling, or transporting alcoholic beverages had been illegal in the United States for six years, any miner worth his salt knew where to obtain locally produced "moonshine." The other missing worker was simply late. The miners commented to each other that he would be lucky if the boss let him stay when he arrived instead of sending him home without pay. As it turned out, the man with the hangover and the man who was late were very lucky indeed.

Leaving the morning light behind, the crew rode down into the gloomy shaft. At about 1,000 feet the corridor branched out in passageways that led to small rooms, or "pockets." Up above, the men operating the cable let it out the full 2,800 feet, depositing a group of miners at the bottom of the shaft. Each man had his station, and soon they were engrossed in their work. The steady hum of the ventilating fan was punctuated by the sounds of cutting and drilling.

On May 27, 1925, people who had time to read the newspaper got an update on explorer Roald Amundsen's expedition to the North Pole. Other articles covered the indictment of high school teacher John T. Scopes of Tennessee, charged with violating state law by teaching Charles Darwin's theory of evolution. By 9:30 A.M. the residents of Coal Glen were going about their daily tasks. Children played games, laughed, and chased each other. The man who had overindulged in corn liquor the night before kept on sleeping. The miner who showed up late for work was sent home by mine supervisor Howard Butler.

Down in the shaft, work continued. Every now and then, in order to expose more coal, a miner would drill holes in the rock and place charges of blasting powder in them. These charges, or "shots," were highly effective when they worked properly. Unfortunately, as miners were well aware, there were no guarantees. Sometimes, instead of exploding into the rock as it was supposed to do, a shot blew out. When this happened, gas or coal dust in the air could be ignited—with fatal results.

Out in the cotton fields, seven-year-old Margaret Wicker played in the dirt with a friend while her family chopped cotton. Her father did not work in the mine, but he was often hired to cut crossties and timbers for the company. Miners occasionally boarded with the Wickers, and Margaret knew many of them. She never forgot the morning of May 27.

"All at once, we heard this big noise, like *boooooom!*" she recalled many years later. "Black and yellow smoke began rolling into the sky. It just got plum dark, black like night, with all that black dust and smoke. All the women started screaming and hollering."

Supervisor Butler jumped from his chair and grabbed a special telephone that connected his office with the mine shaft. The miner who answered the call was working below 1,800 feet. "Things are okay here," he told Butler, adding that he thought the explosion had come from where the shaft spread out into separate passageways.

Butler hung up the telephone and raced to the mine entrance. He and Joe Richardson, a machinist, headed down into the shaft. At 1,200 feet a pile of fallen stone and crushed timber blocked their path. Six men were trapped under the debris, some still alive. They were so blackened with grime, Butler did not recognize any of them.

Up in the cotton field, Margaret Wicker watched, terrified yet fascinated. "People were just hollering and screaming and going every which way," she recalled.

Butler and Richardson had just dragged the injured men to the main shaft when a second explosion rattled their teeth. They were headed for the surface to get help when a third blast roared through the tunnels like a tornado. Butler flung himself on the ground. A rushing wind swept him forward, ripping his cap and lamp from his head and his glasses from his eyes. Barely conscious, he crawled on hands and knees to the opening of the mine. He and Richardson both emerged alive.

At first, clouds of dense, poisonous yellow gas and fumes prevented rescuers from getting close to the mine entrance. The ventilation fans kept whirling, and before long, search parties were able to go in. Wives, children, and other relatives of the miners gathered around the opening.

Numbed by shock and dread, they were largely silent. In the words of a reporter for the Raleigh *News and Observer,* "They whispered together in hopeless monotones and waited. . . . Aged mothers stared with dry eyes and little children tugged at their skirts."

Hours passed. People from the surrounding areas began to arrive to see what was happening. Workers erected a "corral" of ropes and wires to prevent onlookers from getting too close. Word passed among the crowd that fire was burning beyond the wall of crumbled slate and timber. Every time a mine car came to the surface, the crowd leaned forward anxiously. Time and time again they were disappointed. The cars were loaded with debris.

Relief agencies and military personnel at nearby Fort Bragg responded quickly to news of the disaster. Workers from the Cumnock mine across the river came running. The U.S. Bureau of Mines sent experts and rescue cars. Western Union sent extra operators to Sanford, the most logical place from which to communicate with the outside world.

While the crowd's attention was focused on the search for survivors, a few men erected an army tent inside the roped-off area. In somber silence they set up sawhorses and placed pine boards across them. They knew a temporary morgue would be needed.

Daylight faded to dusk; dusk became night. A last-quarter moon appeared in the sky, half light, half shadow. At 10 P.M., soldiers were called to bring stretchers close to the shaft. The six men almost saved by Butler and Richardson had been found. A reporter for the *Charlotte Observer* wrote: "As the cars appeared, the bodies, save for a begrimed hand, cold in death, were not visible, as a merciful tarpaulin had been spread over them." Howard Butler was not there to witness the sight. He had been taken to a hospital in Sanford.

By 1:30 the next morning, mine officials and rescuers knew that no one in the shaft could possibly have survived. Even if the explosions had not killed them, they had certainly succumbed to the mixture of noxious gases that remained. An elderly miner who had served at the Cumnock mine explained the situation to a reporter: "Afterdamp got them this time. It just hits you after the explosion and you fall asleep and never wake up. They say it's easy death and it catches you before you know it."

The next day, at 1,700 feet, workmen caught a glimpse of a gruesome scene: a row of bodies piled in a heap. They had been thrown there by the second and third explosions. Newspapers reported a mass of 5,000 people gathered around the shaft, watching and waiting. In the front line the miners' families continued their calm vigil. That afternoon, more of the dead were removed from the mine. Unable to maintain her stoic demeanor any longer, a woman became hysterical when given a watch that had been on the wrist of one of the victims. Another woman fainted and was carried to the canteen set up by the Red Cross.

Not long after that, two agitated members of an eight-man search crew appeared suddenly at the mine entrance. "Get out!" one of them yelled back into the shaft. "Hurry! The air is bad!"

Anxiety rippled through the crowd, intensifying when the other six workers failed to appear. Just as panic started to break out, the men emerged with two more bodies. They had delayed their exit in order to remove brothers George and Shubert Anderson, found with their arms wrapped protectively around each other.

A representative from the Bureau of Mines took a canary into the shaft to check the air. After an hour's stay in the lower levels, the bird showed no ill effects. Another search team went down. J. M. Hudson, brother of Joe and Dan, was interviewed by the *Fayetteville Observer* on May 28. He had not slept for forty-eight hours. He was a miner, too, but swore those days were over. "I'll never go in again for pay," he vowed.

On Friday, scarcely 300 yards from the shaft, a pastor recited scripture and offered comforting words over the remains of four local

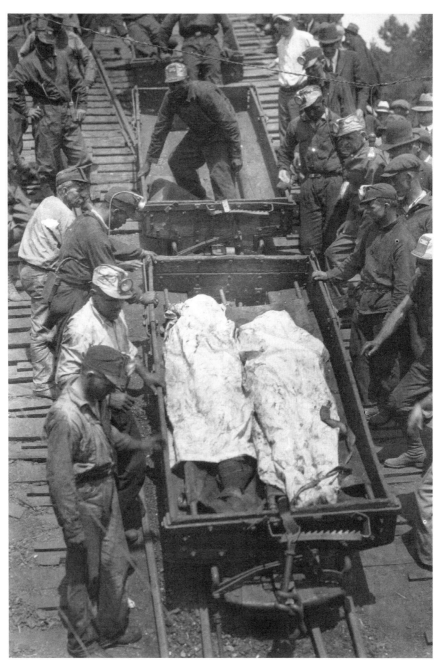

"As the cars appeared, the bodies, save for a begrimed hand, cold in death, were not visible, as a merciful tarpaulin had been spread over them." North Carolina Collection, University of North Carolina Library at Chapel Hill/Ben Dixon McNeill

men. Those who attended the graveside service had to strain to hear his voice over the drone of the huge ventilating fan.

In the bright heat of that afternoon, it was clear that no one would be "rescued." There would be no shouts of triumph as a coal-blackened survivor was pulled from the shaft. Yet heroism was still alive. The men who risked their lives in the depths of Coal Glen mine did so for the sake of those who were left behind—the wives and children and parents, the sisters and brothers. Jeter Adcock, who had never been in the mine, agreed to join a search party. "A small boy came over and told me his father was in the mine and begged me help," Adcock recalled later. "That broke me down."

Embalmers worked day and night without rest, struggling to clean and prepare unrecognizable bodies covered with coal dust and grease.

Relief agencies provided free food, first aid, and supplies to the living victims. The abundance of sightseers attracted less desirable elements to the scene as well. Entrepreneurs set up hot-dog stands. Bootleggers attempted to ply their trade and were ousted or jailed by the sheriff. To the disgust of one *Charlotte Observer* reporter, miners were forced to snatch quick naps on hard boards laid on the ground while "the available sleeping places . . . were well taken up by college boys who came over to lend their valued services toward gumming up the situation."

On Saturday, May 30, a movie producer from Chicago arrived. The Raleigh *News and Observer* noted that he "undertook to tell some of the officers where to head in. They quietly told him where to head out, and he headed, bleating as he went."

That afternoon at 2 P.M., Joe Hudson's mutilated form was transported to the surface in a mine car. A headline in the *Charlotte Observer* the next day declared: "53rd and Last Body Taken from Carolina Coal Mine—Joe Hudson Last of Dead To Be Found." Hudson's father told a reporter: "There's no use being sorrowful, and besides, the women folks have got to be helped out. I believe that God Almighty fixes the time. . . . We all have to come to it some time."

One can only imagine the thoughts of the man whose hangover prevented him from reporting to work that morning and the miner who arrived late and was sent home by the supervisor.

In the aftermath of the Coal Glen disaster, individuals and organizations across the state responded with donations. They met and exceeded the $35,000 amount requested by the Red Cross and the mayor of Pittsboro, county seat of Chatham County. Merchants sent clothing to survivors when they learned that many of them had nothing to wear to the funerals of their loved ones.

A report prepared for the Department of Labor placed the blame for the initial blast on "a blown-out shot" which "ignited the gas and coal dust, resulting in a general explosion throughout the mine, which wrecked the underground ventilating system." Possible explanations for the subsequent explosions were offered. The general condition of the mine was rated "very good with the exception of some coal dust in some of the entries." At the end of the report was a list of rules designed to prevent future disasters.

The Carolina Coal Company went bankrupt in 1930. Mining was attempted along the Deep River in subsequent years, but tragedy continued to plague the efforts. Rumors spread that the mines in the area were jinxed. Geologists offered a different explanation for the difficulties: abundant, highly explosive natural gas; faults in the coal seams; and a dip in the contour of the coal bed that made it hard to reach. Coal Glen mine was closed permanently in 1952.

CHAPTER 11

Gathering Storm

THE AUGUST FLOODS

— 1940 —

AT FIRST THE AUGUST RAIN — COURTESY OF A COASTAL
hurricane — was a welcome sight to the people of Watauga County,
North Carolina. In 1940 most of its 18,000 inhabitants relied on fishing, hunting, cutting timber, and farming to keep food in their stom-
achs and a roof over their heads. Rain fed the rivers and helped
sustain trees, wild game, crops, livestock, and human beings.

Named for the Watauga River, the county was located in the Blue
Ridge Mountains in the northwestern part of the state. *Watauga* was

*On August 14, 1940, relentless rain and a broken dam caused the Watauga River
to flood several towns and communities near the Tennessee–North Carolina line.
This scene, photographed in Wilkes County, illustrates the extent of the damage.*
Photo is from J.J. Andrews collection at James Larkin Pearson Library, Wilkes Community College.

said to derive from a Native American word meaning "beautiful water." The county had long been a destination for people who wanted to escape the heat and disease of the flatlands. In the 1800s, Blowing Rock had become one of the South's first resorts. Before that, Daniel Boone had spent considerable time in the area hunting, hiking the hills, exploring the caves, and drinking clean, fresh water from the creeks and streams. The county seat was named Boone in his honor.

On August 5, 1940, when the rain began to fall, the residents of Deep Gap, Stony Fork, Dutch Creek, and other sections of Watauga County saw no reason to be worried. They were immersed in work, school, family, church, and community activities. Local newspaper accounts of the New York World's Fair were far more interesting than the weather, especially the stories of exhibits featuring the latest wonders of technology: television, nylon stockings, and a robot that could talk and puff a cigarette. For entertainment, a person could tune in to radio programs that brought the voices of Frank Sinatra and Wee Bonnie Baker (Evelyn Nelson) into the mountain coves and hollows. Gene Autry's *Melody Ranch* was a popular radio show.

The war in Europe also occupied many people's thoughts. Adolf Hitler had been appointed as chancellor of Germany seven years before. Those who were listening with their hearts and minds heard the rumble of distant thunder. Storm clouds gathered steadily, building and spreading, casting a dark shadow over Europe and beyond. In 1939 Hitler's Nazis had taken over Czechoslovakia and invaded Poland. That September Britain, France, Australia, New Zealand, and Canada had declared war on Germany.

The United States had tried to remain neutral. In July 1940 the Germans—now supported by Italy—had bombed British airfields and ports. The president of the United States, Franklin D. Roosevelt, had promised support for Britain and its allies in the form of weapons and supplies. Americans were debating whether the country should initiate the first peacetime military draft in its history.

Tuesday, August 6, 1940 dawned drab and gray in Watauga County. Rain continued intermittently during the week and throughout the weekend. On August 11 a hurricane struck Savannah, Georgia, and Charleston, South Carolina. The storm system moved inland, and on the evening of August 13, the rain suddenly started to come down harder in Watauga and the surrounding region. Water began to rise swiftly in creeks and streams. Rocks and clumps of mud loosened by the driving rain began to slide down the hillsides. Before long, landslides covered the roads.

Deep Gap residents Andrew and Eliza Greene gathered in their living room with their five youngest children. As rain hammered the windows and walls, Creola, age sixteen, read a Bible verse aloud. The youngest child, seven-year-old Bennet (called "B.L."), said a little prayer his mother had taught him. Frightened by the storm, Vernita, age twelve, covered her face. Her fourteen-year-old sister, Velma Lea, and brother Hooper, nineteen, gazed out the window. All they could see was muddy water. Suddenly something big and powerful hit the house. A table flew against the wall. An oil lamp, the family's only source of light, crashed to the floor.

Guy Carlton of Deep Gap was alarmed by the water rising steadily around his home. He moved his wife and four children up the road to a service station he owned. They were joined there by Carlton's mother-in-law, Martha Carroll; Lula Anderson, an employee; and Lula's nine-year-old brother, Johnnie. Johnnie sat on a quilt on the station floor crying, afraid of the water and noise.

"We heard the slide rumbling like thunder when it started from the mountain top about a mile above us," Carlton later told the *Watauga Democrat,* "but were trapped in the building by high water. We hoped the slide would go down the hollow to the west of us."

Not too far away, at Stony Fork, Worth Greene, his wife, Lucy, and their twenty-two-month-old daughter, Betty, had stopped at Zeb Vance Greene's house for a visit. With them was Nina Todd, Lucy's fifteen-year-old cousin. As the storm continued, Zeb mentioned that it might be a good idea to move his hogs to a safer place. He, Nina, and Worth stepped onto the front porch to get a better look at what was happening. They were greeted by the loud, steady roar of the rain and the sight of water rising swiftly on all sides. Lightning flashed. The wind howled. Before Zeb and his visitors could decide what to do next, a huge wave swept over the porch.

All across Watauga and adjoining counties, great chunks of earth broke loose from the mountain sides, causing the ground to shake, making a noise that would later be described as "somewhat like continuous thunder except that it was louder and more of a 'whizzing' sound." The rain and wind uprooted trees and sent them tumbling downhill accompanied by logs, huge stones, and masses of earth. These avalanches gathered more trees, rocks, fences, and buildings on the way down. Lightning shot up and down the paths of destruction, creating a strobe effect. Water gushed over the banks of creeks, streams, and river branches and raced in torrents across fields, roads, and private property.

Not long after Andrew Greene's oil lamp broke, an avalanche knocked his house off its foundation. With the family still inside, the structure turned end over end three times, then fell apart. Borne along by the rushing current, nineteen-year-old Hooper soon lodged in a bush. He could see nothing in the stormy darkness but heard his fourteen-year-old sister, Velma Lea, scream as the floodwaters carried her past him. Their mother, Eliza, surrounded by floating debris, struggled to keep her head above water. The limbs of a small tree snagged her clothes and brought her to a halt in the sand. She could still hear the terrifying groan of the landslides all around her. Fearful of being buried, she crawled up onto a higher pile of rubble.

B.L. Greene, age seven, found himself in a drift of logs and other debris. The rain was beating down, so he covered himself with pieces of lumber. He peered out at the night, its blackness broken by pretty, flashing lights. He could hear his mother's voice calling out somewhere above him.

Guy Carlton's hopes of evading a landslide were dashed as a huge slide struck his station with full force. Everyone in the building was thrown across the road. Carlton's mother-in-law was pinned by rocks and dirt. He pulled her out and took her to a nearby shed where she would be protected from the elements. Otis Watson, who owned a service station on the other side of the road, happened to be nearby. He helped carry three of Carlton's children to the shed. Faint cries for help alerted him to the location of the fourth child, a nine-year-old girl.

Nearly blinded by the pounding rain, Watson made his way down a muddy, slippery hill. He found the child lodged between two tree limbs, half-drowned. As he struggled to free her, he worried that she might not survive. Her skin was cold and clammy from the chilly air and water. Finally he got her loose and carried her to the shed where the other rescued victims huddled.

At Zeb Vance Greene's place in Stony Fork, Worth Greene clung desperately to the post that had just saved his life. Right after the wave washed Zeb and Nina off the porch, some peculiar force had pressed Worth against the wall of the house. A few seconds later, he too was pulled toward the raging stream, but he managed to grab onto the post, which kept him from being swept away. Amazingly, the house stood firm, and Worth was able to transfer his grip to the branches of a cedar tree that stood near the steps. "Lucy!" he called to his wife, who was still inside with their baby. "Lucy, stay up there. I'm safe!"

Eliza Greene sat on a mound of branches and debris under an apple tree. When the floodwaters began to recede, she thought she might be able to make it to her Uncle George's house. However, after taking a few steps, she sunk into deep sand. She returned to her drift. A few times she caught sight of Uncle George and called to him, but the wind and rain drowned out her voice. Disheartened, she settled in for the night. She did not realize that her little boy, B.L., was only about 50 yards below her. He, too, had decided not to try to go anywhere until daylight.

Guy Carlton and his family went to a neighboring home. His mother-in-law and the nine-year-old daughter who had been lodged in tree limbs were severely injured. Carlton's employee, Lula Anderson, had nearly broken her back, had lost two toes, and was covered with cuts and bruises. No one had been able to locate her brother Johnnie.

As soon as the floodwaters retreated sufficiently, Worth Greene climbed down from his tree and hurried into Zeb Vance Greene's house. He, Lucy, and baby Betty managed to get to L. M. Cook's home, where other refugees from the storm had gathered. They were all concerned about Lucy's mother, Bessie, a widow who lived with her twenty-six-year-old son, Joe, and four younger children.

The morning of August 14 dawned dismally gray, but the rain had subsided. Eliza started for Uncle George's house. Another relative saw her and waded out to meet her. She collapsed and was taken to L. M. Cook's.

Meanwhile, little B.L. Greene was more than ready to go home. He started out, sloshing through water up to his chest at times. When debris blocked his way, he clambered up a rough bank. His hands and feet were so cold, he wanted to cry, but still he trudged on. When he reached the place where his house should have been, all he found were several chickens, an injured cow, and a pony named Dan who could barely move. Stunned, B.L. stood shivering in his thin shirt, wondering what to do. He supposed he could take refuge in the chicken house. However, as he gazed across the swollen creek at his grandparents' home, he knew that was where he wanted to be.

The heavy rains of August 1940 created disastrous conditions for people in several states. This picture was taken in Wilkes County, North Carolina. Photo from J.J. Andrews collection at James Larkin Pearson Library, Wilkes Community College

B.L. walked along until he came to a place where a tree had fallen across the stream. It was not a very thick tree, but he thought it might work. He climbed on and began crawling on his hands and knees, gritting his teeth as he inched along. The rough bark scraped his briar-scratched legs and it was hard to grip the tree with his stiff, cold fingers. He was almost to shore when he felt the trunk lurch under him.

His grandparents, Rebecca and B. F. Greene, had no idea their grandson was trying to get to their house. They were busy taking care of Bessie Greene and her five children. The widow had been awakened during the night when a large fence rail burst through a window over her bed. The house was picked up, carried about 200 yards, and lodged behind the trunk of a fallen maple tree, about 6 feet in diameter. Bessie's fifteen-year-old son James (J.C.) never forgot the experience. Years later, at age eighty, he still remembered everything "as if it had happened yesterday."

"I woke when the chimney fell on the tin roof," he recalled. "I could feel the house move. I looked out the window and saw the house had turned half around, so it was facing northeast instead of south. I ran downstairs. The water was knee-deep down there."

Bessie and her children managed to make their way up a hill, through the woods, and down treacherous paths in the driving rain. The earth shook under their feet as boulders the size of automobiles banged into each other. At one point Bessie's eldest son, Joe, observed, "It looks as if we are going to be destroyed any way we go." Fortunately he was wrong.

Once the frightened family was safe and warm again, the terror of their experience subsided and they realized they were hungry. Bessie and Rebecca went to the kitchen to prepare breakfast. While they were working, Rebecca glanced out the window. What she saw nearly caused her to drop the dish she was holding. Coming down the hill next to the house was little B.L. His grandmother shouted his name, and everyone ran out to meet him. He was caked with mud and his body was scraped and bruised. Nevertheless, his blue eyes shone with the excitement of his adventure.

"Something had hit him in the mouth," J. C. Greene recalled years later. "It was all puffed up. His clothes had all been torn off except his little T-shirt. He kept talking about the animals and wanting someone to go get the pony that had survived."

The next day, August 15, newspapers across the country headlined the bombing of the British cruiser *Transylvania* in the Atlantic Ocean. London's airport was shelled. A counterattack by English warplanes was launched against the Germans. From Washington came word that some congressmen wanted President Roosevelt to be given authority to call the militia and army reserves to twelve months' active duty "because of the alarming conditions abroad."

Other articles covered the aftermath of deadly floods in Virginia, Tennessee, and the Carolinas. "Heaviest loss of life was centered near the northern end of the Tennessee–North Carolina line," reported the International News Service. "A broken dam sent a 27 foot wall of water roaring down an already swollen Watauga river through several towns and communities."

Eliza Greene lay in a hospital bed, devastated not only by her injuries but by the news that her husband, Andrew, and three daughters had been killed. Her spirits lifted when B.L. was brought into her room. She was relieved that he was alive and safe, even though the bruises and scratches on his face made it hard for her to recognize him. She was grateful that her other two sons, Hooper and Earl, had also survived.

On August 15 the *Watauga Democrat* reported: "A body found in Wilkes county late Tuesday and believed to be that of Nina Todd . . . brings the total count of Watauga's death toll to sixteen." Zeb Vance Greene was listed among the dead. His body, as well as Nina's, had been found in the Yadkin River, buried in the sand of the river bottom. Martha Carroll (Guy Carlton's mother-in-law) lived for two days in the hospital but was finally unable to survive her injuries. Lula Anderson developed pneumonia but eventually recovered. The body of her little brother, Johnnie, was found a few miles from Carlton's service station.

Damage to farmlands was heavy, with the greatest being to corn, hay, and small grain crops. Part of the Linville River railway was washed away. In Watauga County, as elsewhere in the region, relief organizations responded as quickly as possible. The American Red Cross established emergency headquarters in Boone. The North Carolina Board of Charities and Public Welfare delivered food supplies.

The idea of receiving charity did not appeal to some of Deep Gap's residents. The *Watauga Democrat* reported that Otis Watson, "accredited with having pulled nine of the victims from the tons of debris and water which literally fell from the mountainside to cover two residences and two filling stations on the road," vowed that he would not accept aid. "The Lord knows," he said, "I'd rather have been washed away than to be on the relief."

On October 5 the Red Cross closed its office in Boone, having offered help to 220 families in Watauga County. Food, clothing, and sometimes even pieces of furniture and material for small repairs were provided.

Over a year later, on December 7, 1941, the storm clouds of war burst over America when the Japanese bombed Pearl Harbor, Hawaii. More than 2,200 Watauga County residents served during World War II. In nearly four years of service, Hooper Greene received four bronze battle stars as well as other medals and, most important to him, the Victory Medal.

Four decades after the war, in *The Heritage of Watauga County, North Carolina,* Hooper wrote about the flood of 1940 and the deaths of his father and three sisters. In the same publication were a few comments from Betty Greene Norris—the baby who had been visiting Zeb Greene with her parents when the floodwaters swept Nina Todd and Zeb away. She did not remember the events of that terrifying day but had often been told about how her father, Worth, jumped up in a tree to keep from drowning and her mother, Lucy, kept her safely upstairs until the worst of the storm was over.

CHAPTER 12

Like a Bad Dream

THE ATLANTIC COAST LINE WRECK

— 1943 —

JUST BEFORE NOON ON DECEMBER 15, 1943, THE engineer of the Atlantic Coast Line's train number 91 blew two long notes on the horn. The streamliner chugged out of New York's Penn Station hauling eighteen cars: two express cars, a mail car, a passenger-baggage car, five coaches, two dining cars, a tavern car, a lounge car,

At about 1:30 A.M. on December 16, 1943, one ACL "Champion" smashed into another near Buie. Rescuers braved snow and subfreezing temperatures to save as many victims as possible. ACL Photo/William E. Griffin Jr. Collection

and five Pullman sleeper cars. George Pullman had introduced the "sleeper" back in 1865.

The train was called the Tamiami Champion. The name "Champion" had been chosen from over 100,000 entries in a national contest. Officials swore the choice was unrelated to the fact that a man named Champion McDowell Davis was elected president of the Atlantic Coast Line not long after the winning name was chosen. "Tamiami" was a combination of Tampa and Miami.

That crisp morning in December 1943, train number 91 was southbound for Tampa. Its brilliant purple, silver, and yellow color scheme complemented the holiday wrapping paper on the packages carried by many passengers.

William Wood, publisher of the magazine *Small Homes Guide,* settled into his seat with a newspaper, eager to read about the upcoming playoff game between the Washington Redskins and New York Giants. Across the aisle, Captain P. W. Allen, a Navy officer, was engrossed in a copy of *Here Is Your War* by Ernie Pyle.

The war described in Pyle's book had begun back in 1939 in Europe. Germany, Italy, and Japan (the Axis) had signed a pact to support each other. Britain, France, Australia, and New Zealand (the Allies) had declared war on Germany. The United States initially maintained neutrality, but that changed on December 7, 1941, when Japanese planes bombed Pearl Harbor in Hawaii, catapulting Americans into battle.

In 1943 the Allies saw tremendous progress in their fight against the Axis powers. However, victories were won at high cost, and the war was far from over. As the December holiday season approached, Americans were keenly aware that many of their loved ones would spend these special days far from home.

Train number 91 thundered through the countryside, and before long, Washington, D.C., and Petersburg, Virginia, were behind it. More than likely, music from someone's radio floated through the

The engine pictured here is identical to those involved in the disastrous wreck at Buie in December 1943. The name "Champion" was chosen in a national contest. Collection of Harold K. Vollrath

coaches. Passengers may have hummed along with popular crooner Bing Crosby, who had recently recorded "I'll Be Home for Christmas." Written by Kim Gannon, Buck Ram, and Walter Kent, the song went straight to the hearts of military men and women and their families.

Later that day, December 15, another Tamiami Champion—train number 8—pulled out of Miami, headed north. Three streamlined diesel-electric units pulled sixteen cars: a passenger-baggage car, two coaches, a dining car, and a dozen Pullman sleeping cars. Train number 8 was bound for New York. Like the passengers on southbound train number 91, the people going north carried gifts tied with ribbons and talked excitedly about the latest news and their plans for the holidays.

Among the passengers were a large number of soldiers and sailors, many of them on their way home for Christmas. Others had different reasons for traveling. Lt. Edmee Hewitt of the Women's Army Corps (WAC) was on her way to Fort Monmouth, New Jersey. She had been transferred there from Daytona Beach, Florida. Private Martin A. Tessler, who got on the streamliner in Charleston, South Carolina, was planning to spend a three-day pass in Washington, D.C.

Actress and opera singer Grace Moore and her husband, Valentin Parera, had been on the road a lot lately. Moore, known as the Tennessee Nightingale, had made her debut on Broadway in 1920. Now she was devoting much of her time to performing at bond rallies, benefits, and army camp shows. Another passenger, William C. Bullitt, had been America's first ambassador to the Soviet Union. He was traveling north with his daughter Anne. The trip marked the end of a well-deserved rest in Florida following Bullitt's losing campaign for mayor of Philadelphia.

At mealtime the dining cars on both the northbound and southbound Tamiami Champions were full. Because of the war, most trains had cut back on the number of dining cars, variety of foods, and level of service. The New York Central line had even placed an insert in its menus:

> With no additional dining cars being built . . . with some of our present cars busy serving the armed forces . . . the number available for our greatly increased passenger traffic will remain limited for the duration. Many of our chefs, stewards and waiters . . . have exchanged their New York Central uniforms for those of Uncle Sam. . . . From now 'til Victory we will go on serving you to the best of our ability. In the meantime, thanks for your aid and understanding in today's difficult situation.

Just after midnight, train number 91—headed south—made a stop in Fayetteville, North Carolina, departing that station at about 12:25 A.M. on December 16. Some of the passengers were still awake;

many were already asleep, dreaming of awakening in the sunny South-land. As number 91 barreled along at 85 miles per hour, those who peeked out might have been surprised and dismayed to see snow on the ground and sleet pelting the windows.

Less than half an hour later, passengers heard a loud, prolonged *whoosh*. They lurched forward, then back, as the train came to an abrupt halt. Crew members hopped off, wincing at the sting of sharp, icy wind on their faces. They soon saw that the coupling between the second and third cars had broken.

As the crew repaired the broken coupling between the second and third cars, the engineer and baggage men discovered another broken coupling, this one on the front of the first car. They began chaining the car to the engine. They were not concerned about other trains coming along; the Atlantic Coast Line had a modern signal sys-tem that included an automatic train stop. Any other southbound train would be alerted well before it came upon the streamliner undergoing repairs.

What the men working on the first three cars did not realize was that they were looking at only part of the problem. They were unaware that the last three cars had derailed and were stranded about half a mile back. Shortly after the derailment occurred, a flagman on the derailed section had lit a flare and signaled with a white lantern to the crew at the front of the train. He assumed they had seen his sig-nals. They had not.

To make matters worse, two of the derailed cars were partially blocking the northbound side of the parallel tracks. Worried about northbound trains, the flagman headed up the track with fusees, or flares, intending to wave them as a warning.

Back at the stranded cars, a Pullman porter urged passengers to light fires along the track to alert oncoming trains to the danger. Braving the snow, ice, and ten-degree weather, they burned newspa-pers and whatever else they could find.

Forty minutes had passed since number 91's cars derailed. The conductor was trying to contact a dispatcher. He was still unaware that the last three cars had derailed and that two of them were fouling the northward track. The flagman, who was now about 100 feet in front of the engine, realized that he probably should have brought along a supply of torpedoes as an additional precaution. The small explosives could be placed on the track, where they would be fired by the weight of an oncoming train.

Suddenly a familiar sound reached the flagman's ears, and the glare of a headlight punctured the darkness. It was train number 8.

Frank Belknap, engineer of number 8 and a railroad veteran with more than forty-five years of service, had taken control of the train at Florence, South Carolina, at about 12:30 A.M. He was recovering from a serious case of influenza but had been pressed into duty because of a manpower shortage. Belknap later testified that he saw the reflection of number 91's headlight when he was about 4 miles away. As he drew closer, he saw a stationary red light immediately in front of the stalled locomotive but no indication that he should stop.

Horrified by the sight of the oncoming train, number 91's flagman tried to light his fusee. He slipped in the snow and dropped it. The flare was ruined. Frantic, he swung his red and white lanterns at arm's length across his side of the track. Number 8 blew by him at top speed.

A passenger standing in the half-mile gap between the front portion of number 91 and the derailed cars picked up a lamp and swung it as number 8 approached. Other passengers scrambled to safety atop an embankment. Engineer Belknap saw the swinging lamp. In the same moment he saw something that chilled his blood: Two cars leaned at an angle across his track—dead ahead.

At 1:30 A.M. on December 16, 1943, train number 8 slammed into number 91's stranded cars. A shrieking, grating sound accompanied the thunderous roar of metal crumpling metal. On impact, train number 8's diesel-electric units and first eight cars leaped the track and folded together like an accordion. One coach ploughed into a 7-foot embankment beside the track; a second piled up almost directly on top of it; a third telescoped into one end of the second coach.

For a few seconds, silence hung frozen in the icy blackness. Then shouts and cries of pain and terror pierced the air.

William Wood described the experience to reporters later: "You have never seen such a smashup. Coaches were shattered like matchboxes. Bodies were mangled, rails twisted into hairpins and loops all over the place. It was like a bad dream, filled with screams. Their voices echoed and re-echoed in the night." Wood and Captain Allen made their way through the wreckage, trying to locate the injured. "We got blankets from the Pullman cars and hot coffee and whisky from the diner," he said, "then made fires on the snow-covered ground."

As snow continued to fall, Lieutenant Hewitt, the WAC en route to New Jersey, emerged from her sleeping car at the end of the northbound train. Her car had been shaken during the crash but not damaged. After checking on the other WACs, she and another lieutenant waded through heavy slush to the piled-up cars to see if they could help.

The engineer on number 91, William Myers, telegraphed the Atlantic Coast Line office in Rocky Mount, North Carolina. The police soon arrived with a radio transmitter. Help was summoned from every possible direction. The Robeson County coroner, Donnie Biggs, called his son, Chalmers, and told him to pick him up. Biggs had been alerted by the Rocky Mount telegraph operator, who knew the coroner personally and also knew Biggs had an ambulance. Doctors and nurses came from surrounding communities. Their numbers were limited because so many had been sent to Europe to deal with casualties of war.

A reporter from nearby Lumberton later wrote: "First arrivals at the scene told of the injured crying 'Shoot me!' 'Kill me!' and begging for help and water. Scattered about the wreck scene were packages in Christmas wrappings, and broken Christmas toys."

Sixty years later, Chalmers Biggs still remembered his experience vividly. "There were some unbelievable injuries," he recalled. "Massive fractures and cuts and people missing arms and legs. Just horrible."

Military personnel from nearby Fort Bragg and Maxton Air Force Base soon appeared, as did representatives of the Red Cross. Mechanics were summoned to cut through the wreckage with acetylene torches to free trapped victims and uncover the dead. Two Catholic priests who had been on the southbound train administered last rites to passengers who lay dying in the bitter cold.

By dawn on December 16, up to 4 inches of snow had fallen across the deep South, in some places for the first time in decades. At Buie, North Carolina, the location of the wreck, the temperature was only twelve degrees. Slick, snow-covered roads delayed rescuers trying to get to the scene.

Hospitals at Lumberton and Fayetteville received the injured. At Baker Sanitarium in Lumberton, H. M. Baker Sr., the chief surgeon and founder of the hospital, treated patients in every room of the facility, even in the hallways. The medical staff was at half-strength; medical supplies were limited because of the war. Like many physicians in the area, Baker worked steadily into the next day, going without sleep, saving lives and limbs.

Actress and opera star Grace Moore, who had been hurled against the berth above her, later told the *St. Louis Post-Dispatch:* "When the crash came, my husband made sure that I was not seriously injured and then, although he is suffering severely from grippe [influenza], went outside to help wherever he could. Then, for 24 hours we sat in the coach without food or heat."

Victims who were beyond help were taken to morgues and funeral homes. By noon fifty bodies, most of them as yet unidentified, had been taken to a morgue at Red Springs. Local newspapers printed descriptions of physical characteristics and clothing in hopes that relatives would come forward to claim their loved ones.

The Red Cross collected blood from area residents, rushed blood plasma to hospitals, and set up a canteen at the scene of the wreck, where they served coffee and donuts to workers. Inquiry centers in Lumberton and Fayetteville fielded calls from family members and friends.

On December 21 the final death toll was reported: Of the 1,000 people on both trains, 72 had been killed, including 51 servicemen and -women and 21 civilians. More than 120 passengers had been injured. Most of the deaths and serious injuries involved the passengers on the southbound Tamiami Champion.

William C. Bullitt and his daughter Anne were among the survivors. Private Martin A. Tessler was slightly injured. Lieutenant Hewitt received praise from the chaplain of the WAC training center at Daytona Beach, who was also a passenger on the northbound train. "There was no hesitancy about her work among the injured and dying," he said. "She seemed to know what to do and did it."

In the weeks to come, possible reasons for the wreck were hotly debated. An Interstate Commerce Commission investigation presented its findings in a document dated January 18, 1944. According to the commission, the cause of the crash was "Failure to provide adequate protection for derailed cars which fouled an adjacent main track." The commission further noted that it had "received many suggestions for the use of various devices to provide protection for trains under [similar] conditions."

However, the report continued, some of these suggestions "were predicated upon the assumption that members of the crew of No. 91 knew that the rear portion of their train was fouling the northward track." Had the crew at the front of the train made a thorough inspection after the train stopped, the commission pointed out, they would have learned that the rear two cars were obstructing the other track.

On May 8, 1945, Americans celebrated V-E (Victory in Europe) Day. On September 2 that same year, V-J (Victory over Japan) Day was celebrated across the country. Tampa Bay, Florida, commemorated the Japanese surrender with an impromptu street festival, complete with firecrackers and traffic jams. The *Tampa Morning Tribune* reported: "Most effective contribution to the noise making was made by the ACL's Tamiami Champion, outbound . . . with a series of deep-toned hoots."

Even in the midst of celebration, the sound of the train's air horn may have caused more than one listener to recall a snow-covered night in North Carolina back in 1943—a night when the holiday season lost its brightness for many, yet also a night when spirits were buoyed by the unwavering courage, selfless acts, and comforting words of those who came to the rescue.

CHAPTER 13

Princess in a Tower

THE HIGHLAND HOSPITAL FIRE

– 1948 –

TO THE CASUAL OBSERVER, THE WELL-KEPT GROUNDS
and stately structures resembled a college campus. The tennis courts,
swimming pool, and panoramic views of the Blue Ridge Mountains
brought to mind a luxurious resort. However, Oak Lodge, Home-
wood, and the Brushwood bungalow were not part of a university or
grand hotel. Situated on fifty acres of land near the French Broad and

*Of the Central Building's twenty-nine occupants, nine were killed in the fire that
gutted the building on March 10, 1948.* E.M. Ball Photographic Collection [N792G],
D.H. Ramsey Library Special Collections, UNC Asheville 28804

Swannanoa Rivers in Asheville, North Carolina, they were the property of Highland Hospital for Nervous Disorders—an asylum for the mentally ill.

Some of Highland's residents considered the sanitarium a refuge; others saw it as a prison. To the woman sitting in her room in the Central building on March 9, 1948, it was a little of both. She had come to Highland in November 1947, when she could not stop crying, when long walks and prayers no longer brought relief, when she could no longer maintain the guise of normalcy.

This was not her first sojourn in a mental institution. After her first breakdown seventeen years earlier, doctors had diagnosed her with schizophrenia. She had received treatment at several sanitariums, including Highland Hospital. On and off since 1940, she had lived with her mother in Montgomery, Alabama, returning to Highland for short periods of rest and rehabilitation.

During this most recent visit, the woman was undergoing combined insulin and electric shock treatments. She was not responding very well. Her physician described her improvement as "modest." Now, as the woman approached her forty-eighth birthday, she wondered if she would ever feel better again. The answer to that question, when it came, would be unexpected—and unwelcome in the extreme.

For the moment, however, she tried to concentrate on the note she was writing to her daughter, Scottie. The hospital encouraged letter writing, and the woman enjoyed expressing herself, employing a vocabulary that her doctor described as "one of the most extraordinary and beautiful" he had ever encountered. Although remnants of an early-March snowfall still powdered the hospital grounds, the woman chose to focus on the future.

"To-day," she wrote to Scottie, "there is promise of spring in the air and an aura of sunshine over the mountains; the mountains seem to hold more weather than elsewhere and time and retrospect flood roseate down the long hill-sides. . . ."

She might have paused to consider the word *retrospect*. It means looking back, contemplating the past. Even though shock treatments had destroyed some of her memories, she still recalled what it was like to see the world through younger eyes. As a girl she had been courted by many handsome men. One suitor in particular was impossible to forget: a dashing army officer from Minnesota. He had pursued her relentlessly, and they had married in 1920.

Scenes from days gone by passed through the woman's mind, flowing one into another like the view from a slow-moving train. Laughing, eating, dancing, drinking . . . too much, always too much. But after all, it was, in her husband's words, the Jazz Age. The two of them hosted outrageous parties in New York and Paris and mingled routinely with the rich and famous. And why shouldn't they? They were rich and famous themselves: He was F. Scott Fitzgerald, the well-known author, and she was Zelda Sayre Fitzgerald, his beautiful, witty, unpredictable wife. A friend had once commented, "Mr. Fitzgerald is a novelist and Mrs. Fitzgerald is a novelty."

The woman could not help smiling a little, remembering those early days, the decade some people liked to call the Roaring Twenties. Scott had been so romantic, so passionate and possessive. "I used to wonder why they kept princesses in towers," he wrote during their courtship. He had called her his princess, and told her he would like to keep her shut forever in an ivory tower for his own delight.

So much had changed since then. The country had endured a disastrous economic depression and a second world war. The Jazz Age was long gone. Instead of cars that resembled a carriage minus the horse, people drove big, sleek automobiles with long hoods and sloping backs. Instead of knee-length, straight flapper dresses, women wore styles with lower hemlines and shoulder pads, cinched tight at the waist.

As for F. Scott Fitzgerald, he had died of a heart attack in 1940. Now his widow gazed sadly through barred windows at snow-dusted mountains. All of the windows in the Central building were barred as a precautionary measure. In the days to come, that practice would be harshly criticized.

Someone tapped on her door. "Mrs. Fitzgerald?" A nurse entered the room. "It's time for exercise class." For the most part, Mrs. Fitzgerald enjoyed Highland Hospital's regimen, which included gym classes, tennis, and swimming. Patients were required to walk 5 miles a day in the hills surrounding the facility. Recreational and occupational therapy were also on the schedule. Mrs. Fitzgerald took sewing lessons and played bridge. Painting and ballet were among her other interests.

Founded in 1904 by Dr. Robert S. Carroll, Highland Hospital had originally been called Carroll's Sanitarium. In 1939 Dr. Carroll had donated the facility to Duke University. Shortly after that the Central building where Mrs. Fitzgerald lived had been remodeled and now consisted of over 600 feet of porch space, an assembly hall, hydrotherapy and culinary departments, offices, and examination and treatment rooms. Dr. Carroll had retired in 1945, replaced by psychiatrist Basil T. Bennett.

At Highland, diet was restricted. Alcohol, tobacco, and drugs were forbidden. The guiding principle was that nervous disorders could be kept under control by expelling toxins from the body.

Mrs. Fitzgerald and all of the other women receiving insulin and shock therapy were clustered together on one floor. That way, it was easier for the staff to monitor them closely. The women came from different places, including Georgia, Tennessee, North Carolina, and Missouri. Some were quite young, like Miss Borochoff, Mrs. James, and Miss DeFriece, who were in their twenties. Others, such as Mrs. Kennedy, Mrs. Womack, Mrs. Doering, and Mrs. Hipps were closer to Mrs. Fitzgerald's age. At sixty-seven, Mrs. Engle was one of the older residents.

As Mrs. Fitzgerald stepped outside into the chilly morning air, she noticed the grass, its sad, brown color broken by patches of white. Evergreen trees were the only things that kept the grounds from looking completely barren. But, as she had written to Scottie, a "promise of spring" was in the air.

The next day, March 10, the weather improved, with the temperature climbing up to sixty-five. Mrs. Fitzgerald viewed this as a sure sign that spring was imminent. She looked forward to seeing azaleas and dogwoods in bloom, to breathing in perfumed air warmed by the sun.

That night the patients retired to their rooms as usual. Some received medication to induce sleep, including Mrs. Fitzgerald. At 11 P.M., Willie Mae Hall, the night supervisor, came on duty. She went to the top floor of the Central building, where she spoke briefly with nurse Doris Jane Anderson. Before leaving the building, Miss Hall stopped for a few minutes in the main kitchen. By 11:25 she was on her way to Oak Lodge, another building on the Highland campus.

About five minutes later, Miss Anderson went to the kitchen herself. As she drew close, she smelled smoke. Nothing was on fire in the main kitchen, but when she pushed open the door to the diet kitchen, she found the air clouded with a haze that stung her eyes. She saw flames about a foot high around the top edge of a small table.

Later, she would comment that it reminded her of the fiery hoop animals jump through in a circus. She would also admit that she had never been taught how to put out a fire.

Nearly frozen with horror, Miss Anderson could not think clearly at first. Finally she decided she should notify the night supervisor. She ran to her station on the top floor and picked up the telephone. To her dismay, the hospital's private branch exchange was not working. Then, when she asked the central exchange operator to put her through to Oak Lodge, the line was busy. Her next choice was obvious.

"Please connect me to the fire department!" she told the operator. "Hurry!"

Margaret Sledge, a nurse on duty in the Central building, was checking on her patients when she heard a loud thump. A short time later she heard a scraping noise that sounded like the dumbwaiter falling in the shaft that led to the diet kitchen. Glancing out the window, she saw sparks raining down on the porch from above. Mrs. Sledge quickly roused several elderly patients and took them outside. By then, flames were leaping out of the top of the building.

Hospital employees immediately rescued a number of residents who were locked in their rooms due to a history of violent behavior. Miss Anderson led a few patients down the back fire escape of the Central building. That route was soon cut off, literally, as fire consumed the wooden steps and railing.

Two teenagers, Lawrence Mitchell and Kenneth Haynes, were on their way home from a Naval Reserve meeting when they saw a fire engine shoot out of the station, siren wailing. The boys followed the truck to Zillicoa Street, near the north end of Montford Avenue. Black smoke and crackling orange flames billowed from the hospital's roof and windows. Haynes and Mitchell could hear patients screaming above the dull roar of the blaze. They worked with firemen to place ladders against the burning structure.

"We helped four women patients out of the building," Mitchell said later. "And went up a ladder to get an old lady who was standing at a fourth-floor window. She told us to be careful, and came down the ladder by herself when the bars were broken from the window. Boy, she sure was brave."

The teens worked with firemen, hospital staff, and volunteers to remove patients from the back of the building. Made entirely of wood, it was burning faster and more furiously than the front section, which was veneered with stone. The charred odor of burning timbers could be smelled for blocks. Spectators, journalists, and photographers soon assembled. No automobiles were allowed anywhere near the fire, but hundreds of people came on foot, some merely curious, some eager to assist. Reporter Eugene Ray later described the scene:

> A swirling, twisting mass of yellow-colored flame, literally exploding through the roof of Highland hospital's Central building, rose in a fiery 30-foot column. . . . The leaping flames crackled as they were sucked upward through the dumb waiter shaft, mushrooming into the main corridors on the four floors and penetrating through the composition roof. The fire threw out a great light which penetrated to the outer fringes of the gathering, flickering on the faces of those about.

Newsman Al Erxleben was enlisted to help carry a frail blonde woman in a blue-green dressing gown to the administration building. "I felt for a pulse," Erxleben wrote. "Her heart was still beating faintly. I brushed her dingy, soot-covered hair out of her face as nurses and a doctor arrived."

The victim was Mrs. Kennedy of Kinston, North Carolina, who resided on the top floor of the Central building. Artificial respiration and oxygen failed to revive her. Mrs. Hipps, widow of an Asheville physician, was evacuated from that floor as well. In spite of heroic efforts made on her behalf, she did not survive. Dr. P. R. Terry, the coroner, pronounced both Mrs. Kennedy and Mrs. Hipps dead at 2:10 A.M. on Thursday, March 11.

Doctors and nurses arrived from all over the city. Many worked until they were overcome by smoke as they attempted to save as many patients as they could. Hospital director Bennett led rescue operations. Supervisor Frances Bender and assistant supervisor Bettie Ubbenga were later praised for their extraordinary efforts. The Buncombe County Red Cross set up emergency kitchens in nearby homes to provide refreshment to firemen, doctors, nurses, and volunteers. Red Cross drivers transported residents to private homes and other hospitals.

Once removed from the burning building, residents had to be escorted to other locations where staff could care for them. Many patients were saved. Many came out unaided, and some even helped rescue others. Dressed in night clothes and wrapped in blankets, they gathered in the corridors, stairwells, and rooms of adjoining buildings. As the fire raged on, they paced back and forth, unable to ignore the roaring inferno not more than 100 feet away.

According to one newspaper article, a woman with black curly hair asked if anyone had a cigarette lighter or a match. "I don't think it's hardly the time to light a match, dearie," someone said. Hands trembling, the woman shoved her unlit cigarette into the pocket of her housecoat and walked away.

About thirty Asheville firefighters, aided by volunteers from other fire departments, finally brought the blaze under control. The Central hall had been gutted. Blackened timbers leaned at precarious angles against a three-walled shell of stone and twisted steel.

As the sun came up on Thursday the coal supply in the sub-basement boiler room continued to smoulder. Steam, smoke, and fumes swirled upward as firemen probed the rubble for bodies. The first was recovered from the ruins shortly after 8 A.M. The woman could not be identified at that time but was later determined to be Miss Borochoff. Not long after 10 A.M., a diamond ring and wedding band helped identify a second body as that of Mrs. Doering.

Of the Central building's twenty-nine occupants, four were now known to be dead. All had been in rooms on the top floor. Five top-floor residents were still missing.

At noon Thursday the city building inspector halted search and rescue operations. The section of the building where the bodies were thought to be was dangerously weak. Employees from a salvage company worked the rest of the day and into the night removing steel girders and crumbling walls.

Over the next day or two, more bodies were recovered, including those of Mrs. Engel, Miss DeFriece, Mrs. James, and Mrs. Womack. Zelda Sayre Fitzgerald's body was identified by a charred slipper beneath her body and, later, by dental records. The nine women on the top floor were the fire's only fatalities.

"I used to wonder why they kept princesses in towers," Scott Fitzgerald had often said to the beautiful, unpredictable love of his life. Like a princess in a tower, his wife had believed she was safe and secure at Highland Hospital. She had relied on her caretakers to protect her, but in the end, her "tower" had burned to the ground.

The tragedy at Highland Hospital was followed by an inquest and numerous lawsuits on behalf of the dead women. Fire Chief J. C. Fitzgerald (no relation to Scott) testified that if the alarm had been turned in thirty minutes sooner, the fire could have been stopped and no lives would have been lost. The issue of barred windows also came up. An attorney for the plaintiffs declared that state law prohibited barriers on doors and windows in any but a grade "A" hospital building, and that the Central building was grade "C."

On April 1, 1948, the *Asheville Citizen* reported that a Buncombe County coroner's jury had found "there was negligence, but not to the extent to be classed as culpable negligence" in the deaths.

Less than two weeks later, in a bizarre twist, night supervisor Willie Mae Hall walked into Asheville police headquarters and asked to be locked up. When asked why, she replied, "Because I am afraid of what I might do."

Miss Hall told officers: "There are places in Oak Lodge I have picked out that could be set afire. I have thought about it so much I am afraid of what I might do and I want you to lock me up." Asked whether she had set the fire in the Central building, Miss Hall said she could have, but did not think she had. A judge ordered that Miss Hall undergo a psychiatric examination, and she was subsequently hospitalized at a facility in another section of the state. The exact cause of the fire was never determined.

In December 1948 Dr. Robert S. Carroll's daughter, Dr. R. Charman Carroll, replaced Dr. Bennett as director of Highland Hospital. Bennett resigned to become chief neuropsychiatrist at the Veterans Hospital in Nashville, Tennessee. Highland Hospital closed its doors in 1993. Since then, its buildings have served many purposes, and the campus is still a beautiful place. A sunken garden marks the spot where the Central hall once stood. The garden is particularly lovely in the spring.

CHAPTER 14

Everything Was Just Gone

HURRICANE HAZEL

– 1954 –

CERTAIN NAMES BRING TO MIND THE SPIRIT AND
style of America in 1954—for example, Marlon Brando (Academy
Award winner), Patti Page (singer), Linus Pauling (Nobel Prize for
chemistry), Babe Didrikson Zaharias (professional golfer), and
Joseph McCarthy (senator who persecuted suspected Communists).
Dwight D. Eisenhower was president of the United States. Roger
Bannister ran the first four-minute mile. Elvis Presley cut his first
record.

*Hurricane Hazel slashed through buildings all along the Carolina coast. The
Breakers Hotel suffered damage to more than sixty rooms.* Photo by *Wilmington
Star-News*

In October of that year, a storm left a particularly vivid mark on America and other countries as well. Long after the celebrities of the day had passed away, people still recalled the name of that storm. Hundreds of thousands would always remember 1954 as the year Hazel came to town.

The current method of naming hurricanes was initiated in 1953. For several centuries before that, storms in the West Indies were given the names of saints traditionally honored on the days the storms hit (San Ciriaco, Santa Ana). Hurricanes were also identified by latitude and longitude or by the order in which they appeared in a season (Hurricane 1, 2, 3). For a short time the United States used a phonetic alphabet system (Able, Baker, Charlie).

In 1953 the National Weather Service devised a method it hoped would be less confusing. Allegedly taking its cue from the novel *Storm* by George R. Stewart, it began using female names for Atlantic hurricanes. Eight storms were named in 1953, beginning with Alice, followed by Barbara, Carol, Dolly, Edna, Florence, Gail, and Hazel. The next year, the weather service started over again with Alice.

Like warm-up acts for a big-name entertainer, the 1954 versions of hurricanes Carol and Edna played North Carolina just before Hazel arrived. Carol chose August for her performance. Although property damage occurred along the coast, North Carolina was spared the full brunt of the storm. Edna took the stage in September, less than two weeks after Carol. She also passed offshore. Damages in North Carolina were widespread but light. Many North Carolinians thought (or hoped) that was the whole show for the season. They had no idea that Hazel was waiting in the wings.

Hazel got her start October 5 in the southeastern Caribbean sea. Right away she flaunted her talent, demonstrating fancy footwork as she built up speed and zigzagged over the Grenadine Islands. In the early hours of October 11, she turned her attention to Haiti. Her appearance in that country was unforgettable. Torrential rains, winds in excess of 125 miles per hour, landslides, and surge flooding (a rise in water caused by the wind) overwhelmed the island. Estimates on the number of Haitians killed range from 400 to 1,000.

Passing east of the Bahamas, Hazel created a "phenomenal sea," according to an Air Force meteorologist who viewed her from a B-29 bomber. The force of the wind cut the tops off the waves. The ocean was a "continuous mass of whitecaps and frothing foam."

Hazel was on her way to North Carolina, but on Thursday, October 14, that was hard to believe. The skies over Brunswick County were bright blue. A few white clouds sailed high above sparkling beaches. Waves, tipped with just a touch of white, rolled gently to shore. Seabirds dipped into the water for fish and soared back into the sky. To Jerry and Connie Helms, who were honeymooning on Long Beach, and the Register family, who lived on Ocean Isle Beach, it was a pleasant fall day. Rain and cooler weather was forecast because of the hurricane, but that was seen as good news for drought-ravaged counties in eastern and central North Carolina.

Jerry and Connie Helms went roller-skating in a neighboring town on Thursday night, October 14. While they were gone, police went door to door on Long Beach advising people that a hurricane was approaching and they should evacuate. At his home on Ocean Isle, Sherman Register heard about the storm. His brother-in-law encouraged him to leave, but Register just laughed. "Those weather people make a lot out of nothing," he said.

Jessie Taylor of Southport would have taken exception to his remark. The seventy-four-year-old woman was one of the weather bureau's volunteer observers and the daughter of a professional weather forecaster. What she had seen and heard of Hazel troubled her deeply. She picked up her telephone the evening of October 14 and started calling people in Fort Caswell, Long Beach, Holden

Beach, and Ocean Isle. F. C. Simmons, a weather service volunteer in Shallotte, did likewise. Their message to everyone they reached was the same: "Get out *now!*"

Advisories went out by radio, television, and newspaper. Public and emergency agencies were notified. Storm warnings were displayed along the coast. In 1954 there were no satellites, and little if any information was provided on storm surge. Not every person living along the coast had television or even radio. Some had no telephone. In many cases it was up to local law enforcement officers to warn residents in person.

By dawn on October 15, Hazel was on the coast and moving fast. At Long Beach the Helmses awoke to the sounds of roaring wind and churning waves. Their cottage, which belonged to Connie's parents, had been several hundred feet from the sea, with high sand dunes between the house and the water. Now Connie could see the ocean billowing above the dunes. Without a telephone or television, the Helmses had to rely solely on their own observations. They decided to leave as quickly as possible.

Over on Ocean Isle Beach, the Register family had a similar rude awakening. Seeing water everywhere, Sherman Register, his wife, and their two children took refuge in a larger house. When that began to fall apart, they and seven other people swam through breakers to a pickup truck. The women and children climbed in while the men struggled to keep the truck upright. Teenager Sonja Register and her younger brother, Buddy, huddled in the truck bed with their neighbors, terrified by the howling wind, driving rain, and the sights and sounds of an ocean gone mad.

Between 9:30 and 10:00 A.M. on October 15, the center of the storm struck near the North Carolina–South Carolina border. By then it was a Category 4 hurricane. Not until Hurricane Hugo in 1989 would a storm of such intensity batter the Carolinas.

The Helmses jumped into their car but it would not start. "We started seeing houses exploding then floating away," Jerry Helms recalled. "Sometimes you could see the whole house flying through the air. At one time a house came straight toward us, and we thought *Oh Lord, this is it*." The couple waded through waist-deep water to a nearby two-story home. Pulling themselves up a handrail on an outside staircase, they broke through a door on the second floor. Before long the floor buckled. All illusions of safety vanished.

Connie Helms could not swim. Jerry could, but wondered if he was any match for the angry waves. The newlyweds tore a blanket and tied one section of it around Connie. They pushed a mattress through a window and Connie climbed aboard. Holding the other end of the blanket strip, Jerry jumped into the water. "We were just swept right away," he said later. Soon all the two-story houses were covered by water. The Helmses held on to their blanket and mattress, determined to stay alive.

On Ocean Isle a huge breaker washed over the pickup truck in which Sonja Register and the others had sought refuge. Her father grabbed the teenager's mother and brother, but Sonja was swept away. Although she was a good swimmer, the surf was so choppy she could barely keep her head above the waves. She saw nothing but water all around her. *Oh Lord help me*, she thought, *I'm going out to sea.*

The exceptionally high floodwaters were due in part to the storm's timing. Hazel hit during a full moon, during the highest lunar tide of the year. As a result, the storm surge was up to several feet higher than it would otherwise have been.

As Hazel headed inland she was expected to lose intensity. In Goldsboro, about 125 miles north and well inland from the beach, schools started on schedule Friday, October 15. Before morning was very far along, however, the principal of Walnut Street School learned that Hazel was not behaving according to expectations. The wind had

A home collapses into a new cut in the dunes between the ocean and the Carolina Beach Lake following Hurricane Hazel, as shown in this photo taken October 10, 1954. Photo courtesy Dwight Ratts

knocked five school buses off the road. Now the hurricane, still dangerously forceful, was coming right over Goldsboro.

Parents were notified to come and get their children. To protect the students and prevent panic, the music teacher at Walnut Street gathered 800 youngsters in the auditorium for a songfest. "We sang and sang," the teacher later recalled. "And ever so often, someone would come up and tap children on the shoulder and they'd leave."

Even further inland the Winston-Salem Fair and Dixie Classic Livestock Show was not going well. To the dismay of fair manager James Graham, Hazel blew down the "big top," sending chickens squawking, lambs bleating, and cows bellowing in every direction. A trained monkey escaped and sought asylum in a nearby house. Already unnerved by the violent storm, the homeowner shrieked in alarm as the agitated simian jumped across her furniture.

In the Raleigh area the wind reached nearly 100 miles per hour. Tornadoes blew down two or three trees per block. Power lines were tangled and broken. Electricity went off. Telephones went out.

Hazel's eye brought an end to rain. Clouds grew thinner, with little or no wind. These conditions lasted about twenty to thirty minutes. Then, with a terrible roar, a huge, ugly bank of black clouds moved in. The wind changed direction, blowing even harder than before.

The coastal areas suffered the worst of Hazel's rampage. At Calabash in Brunswick County, flooding reached 18 feet above the mean low-water level. Water surged into the basement of the Morehead City Hospital in Carteret County. As fire trucks pumped, nurses working in floodwaters up to their knees struggled to save patients and equipment. At Atlantic Beach an 8-foot storm surge with 20-foot waves crashed through a hotel.

All along the coast, Red Cross disaster crews, civil defense agencies, and state and local authorities mobilized people and equipment to help victims of the storm. Amateur Radio clubs provided emergency communication.

The Helmses kept their heads down, close to the mattress, hoping they would not be hit by flying appliances, shingles, and large timbers. Jerry caught hold of a section of a house that drifted by and pushed the mattress on top of it, hoping to create a sturdier raft. Hazel treated the Helmses to an experience that made the most unnerving thrill ride at any theme park seem tame. She then deposited their makeshift craft in the treetops at the island's leeward side.

Exhausted, cold, and stunned by their ordeal, the couple waited for the flooding to subside. "We couldn't see nothing nowhere," Jerry recalled. "We couldn't hear nothing. We thought we were the only people left in the world." As the waters slowly began to recede, it seemed as though the island was rising out of the ocean. Connie was reminded of the science-fiction movies so popular during the 1950s.

"It was just like we were living in one of them," she recalled. "Everything was flat as a table top; all the dunes, all the houses, everything was just gone."

The Helmses climbed down from the treetops and walked toward Southport, the closest town. Connie's parents had rushed to Long Beach from their home in Whiteville, near Wilmington, to check on the couple. A National Guardsman stopped them, explaining that no one was allowed on the beach. Determined to find her seventeen-year-old daughter, Connie's mother declared, "Well then, I guess you'll just have to shoot me!" Fortunately that was not necessary. Connie and Jerry soon appeared, at which point Connie's mother fainted. After being examined at a hospital, the newlyweds returned with Connie's parents to Whiteville.

According to Sonja Register's aunt, Sonja was unconscious when she was found "in the bushes and trees on the other side of the Inland Waterway." Rescuers broke into a nearby cottage and covered the girl with blankets before taking her to a hospital. Sonja survived. However, her parents and brother perished. Sonja lived with her aunt and uncle until she graduated from college. According to an interview given by her aunt to the Wilmington *Star-News* in 2004, Sonja prefers not to talk about Hurricane Hazel. It is easy to understand why.

Hazel caused 19 deaths and 200 injuries in North Carolina, most of them along the beaches of Brunswick County. Total losses in the state were estimated at $136 million. After tearing past Goldsboro and Raleigh, Hazel blew through Virginia, Maryland, Pennsylvania, Delaware, New Jersey, New York, and even up into Canada, causing power failures, flooding, destruction, and death. She herself did not die until after she had crossed the Arctic Circle en route to Scandinavia. In total, from Haiti to Canada, she took at least 600 lives—perhaps far more—and caused close to $350 million in property damage.

The faces of all the heroes who met Hazel's challenge will forever be remembered by the hurricane's victims. In 1955 the weather bureau honored volunteer observer Jessie Taylor for her efforts to warn people about Hurricane Hazel's proximity and fury that evening of October 14, 1954.

Hurricane experts say it is difficult to measure one storm against another. There are many variables, and results are affected by the type of "measuring stick" used. One way to acknowledge particularly deadly storms is to "retire" their names. Countries devastated by a hurricane can request that the World Meteorological Organization confer this dubious honor on a specific storm. Retiring a name means that it cannot be used for at least ten years.

Not surprisingly, Hazel's "outstanding performance in the role of a hurricane" earned her a place on the list of retirees. Although the name could have been used again as early as 1964, a comeback seems unlikely.

CHAPTER 15

Fallout from a Cold War

THE CRASHES OF TWO
B-52 BOMBERS
– 1961 –

THE CHILL IN THE AIR IN JANUARY 1961 HAD NOTHING
to do with the season and everything to do with world politics. For
fifteen years the Soviet Union had been committed to spreading
Communism worldwide, a position that provoked tension and

military rivalry with the United States. During a congressional debate in 1947, American presidential advisor Bernard Baruch coined an expression that would forever define the icy antagonism that stopped just short of open confrontation: He called it the "Cold War."

By 1950 both countries had nuclear weapons. The United States had used the atom bomb to subdue Japan during World War II. The Soviets exploded their first atomic warhead in 1949. The two nations confronted each other indirectly in the Korean War, which lasted three years and ended with the Asian country still divided into two hostile states. In 1956 Soviet Premier Nikita Khrushchev delivered a threat to the West: "We will bury you!" The Russian words he used could also have been interpreted "We will outlast you." Either way, the message was clear.

To deter attack by the Soviets, America's Strategic Air Command (SAC) ordered B-52 bombers to patrol U.S. airspace twenty-four hours a day. The planes were equipped with nuclear bombs.

The year 1961 began with Fidel Castro, the anti-American dictator of Cuba, accusing U.S. president Dwight D. Eisenhower of plotting to invade his nation. A military parade in Havana featured heavy weapons provided by the Soviet Union. The front pages of American newspapers blared a warning from the United States to Communist China and North Vietnam: "Stay Out of Laos." The small Southeast Asian country was in the midst of a power struggle among neutralist, rightist, and Communist forces.

On January 20 John F. Kennedy took the oath of office as America's thirty-fifth president. Kennedy's inaugural speech emphasized a quest for peace but offered no conciliation to Communism. He declared: "We shall pay any price, bear any burden, meet any hardship, support any friend or oppose any foe in order to assure the survival and success of liberty."

During the Cold War, Seymour Johnson Air Force Base, located near Goldsboro, North Carolina, deployed B-52s carrying nuclear weapons on airborne alert missions. Opened in 1942, the base had been deactivated in 1946, then reopened in 1956 as a Tactical Air Command (TAC) base.

On January 23, 1961, eight soldiers from Seymour Johnson took to the air in a sleek, gray B-52G Stratofortress bomber. They flew east, patrolling the coast, circling over the Atlantic Ocean. Just before midnight Maj. Walter F. Tulloch, the pilot, notified the base that he was having fuel problems and needed to return for an emergency landing. Tulloch and his crew were minutes away from the base when they lost control of the plane.

In the dark skies above the rolling uplands of Wayne County, Tulloch quickly assessed the situation and ordered his crew to bail out. The B-52G had only six ejection seats. Two of the eight men would have to leap from the jet with their parachutes. As the bomber spun wildly upside down, Tulloch and four crew members ejected. A sixth man jumped through an open hatch in the roof. Two soldiers were left onboard.

At 12:30 A.M. on January 24, a farmer near the tiny town of Faro, North Carolina, heard a plane "about half running" overhead. Suddenly a violent explosion shook the farmer's house. "It sounded like *whoom,*" he said later, "then there were four other explosions, not as large as the first."

"I heard the whine of an airplane about to land," another farmer told reporters, "then there was a big explosion. It almost knocked me out of bed. I got up and ran to the window and saw my whole field on fire."

Seven parachutes descended to earth in the pale moonlight. One carried a model MK39 thermonuclear weapon jettisoned before the explosion. A second MK39 fell free, gaining speed as it plummeted toward the earth.

Although the bombs were equipped with interlocking safety systems, Tulloch and his crew could not help wondering if the arming sequences had been accidentally activated during the breakup of the plane. If either of the warheads detonated, homes and other buildings within a 5-mile radius would be leveled. The heat from the blast would probably set fire to everything within a 9-mile radius and inflict third-degree burns. People 12 miles from the crash in any direction would suffer second-degree burns. The men could only hope for the best as they floated in the midnight wind.

The nuclear device carried by parachute hit a group of trees. The lines caught in the branches, jerking the bomb violently, but it landed intact. Years later Robert McNamara, secretary of defense under President Kennedy, stated that the bomb's arming mechanism "had six or seven steps to go through to detonate, and it went through all but one."

The free-falling A-bomb struck an open field at high speed. It buried itself in the soggy ground, creating a crater 8 feet in diameter and 6 feet deep.

Trees collapsed Maj. Tulloch's parachute and he landed hard. Finding swampy terrain every way he turned, he rolled up in his parachute to protect himself from subfreezing temperatures and waited for dawn.

State Patrol officers and teams of radioactivity experts rushed to the scene. Flames shot high into the air from the wreckage, which was scattered over more than a mile and a half of flat, sandy tobacco land. For several hours firefighters from ten rural companies fought to extinguish blazes all around the crash. Their hard work was rewarded. Although the B-52 had fallen within 200 yards of homes on both sides of the area, none of the buildings caught fire.

Four survivors were picked up shortly after rescuers arrived. At daylight Maj. Tulloch emerged from the woodland near the crash site. The bodies of two crewman were found in the wreckage. Tulloch recalled that when he ejected, one of the men was trying to assist the other with his parachute. They had obviously never escaped. A third

The crash of a B-52G Stratofortress bomber near Goldsboro in January 1961 brought firefighters, rescue workers, and military officials on the run. The plane was carrying two nuclear devices. Courtesy of The North Carolina State Archives. Reprinted by permission of the *News & Observer* of Raleigh, North Carolina.

body was found about 2 miles away. Air Force officials speculated that the victim was blown from the plane and killed when it broke up, and that his parachute had opened automatically.

Excavation of the buried bomb began at around 1:30 A.M. on January 24. The presence of an unexploded nuclear device provided ample motivation to move slowly. Freezing weather and water in the hole hampered the effort. Eight feet down, workers recovered a portion of the weapon's main body and pieces of the nose section.

Residents of the Goldsboro area awoke to what they thought was a typical January morning, only to discover they had barely escaped nuclear annihilation. At least that was the impression they got from newspaper headlines such as "Huge Bomber Crashes . . . Air Force Jet Bursts Into Flames Near Goldsboro; A-Weapons Aboard." The press went on to reassure readers that the weapons were "unarmed" and that "there was no immediate danger" according to military officials.

Digging continued for two weeks at the crash site, revealing other pieces of the potentially deadly device. By February 7 the crater was 200 feet in diameter and 42 feet deep. Excavation had to be canceled because of cave-ins, freezing weather, equipment limitations, and rising water, courtesy of the nearby swamp.

The Cold War continued to pervade every aspect of American life. Communities across the country conducted regular atomic-bomb drills. Schoolchildren studied the whys and wherefores of fall-out shelters. In Laos, Communist-supplied soldiers clashed with royal troops. The Laotian government declined an offer by the Southeast Asia Treaty Organization (an alliance between the United States, Australia, France, Great Britain, New Zealand, Pakistan, the Philippines, and Thailand) to intervene in its civil war. B-52s remained on around-the-clock patrol over U.S. airspace.

The news of the crash near Goldsboro was still fresh in everyone's mind at the end of March 1961. On the night of March 30, just before 10 P.M., highway patrolman Ray Kirkman was driving down North Carolina 109 in Davidson County. Suddenly an ear-splitting *boom!* rattled his car. A blinding flash illuminated the dark sky, a flash that was later reported to have been seen 40 miles away. Kirkman, an Air Force veteran, sped south toward the light.

The police chief of the closest town—Denton, North Carolina—looked outside the station window just in time to see an airplane ignite. "It was like dynamite, going up," he said later. "There was a big red and blue flash and the plane just fell apart."

Frances Crouse was sewing in her rural home in Davidson County when she heard the explosion. She thought her front door was going to come off its hinges. "What was that?" she exclaimed. Her husband, Aaron, tried to reassure her. "It's probably just a plane breaking the sound barrier." He was wrong.

A neighbor, John Frank, heard the noise and looked out his window. Across the field from his home, about 150 yards away, raged a fire. He wondered if it signaled the end of the world or the beginning of a war.

About twenty minutes after the explosion, someone knocked on the Crouses' door. Mrs. Crouse answered. "There stood this airman with his helmet under his arm," she recalled later. "He said 'We've had trouble. Do you think you can help me?'"

The man was First Lt. Glen C. Farnham, an electronic-warfare officer from Texas. He had been aboard a B-52G Stratofortress bomber—the same type of plane that had crashed near Goldsboro. Farnham and the other seven crew members on the plane were stationed at Dow Air Force Base in Bangor, Maine. They had been taking part in a refueling exercise. During the refueling approach the B-52 had tilted sharply at an unusual angle. Objects began to fly around inside the bomber. Farnham was unable to read the instruments to determine what was happening. The plane began to fall. "Bail out! Bail out!" shouted the commander.

Farnham later recalled his descent to earth: "The next thing I remember was the chute blossoming. . . . I saw an orange ball underneath me. It might have been the plane. . . . All of a sudden the ground came up awful fast, but I landed in a plowed field, so it wasn't too bad." He got up and started walking toward a farmhouse. "I had a little trouble as I crossed electric wires for cattle and got shocked a couple of times."

Mrs. Crouse insisted that Farnham lie down on a couch in her den. Her husband called the hospital in Denton.

Patrolman Kirkman was the first lawman on the crash scene, a field near Silver Hill Mine Road. All he could see were flames leaping from a crater that looked about 150 feet long by 30 feet wide. He never saw the plane, which was not surprising given that the crater was 30 feet deep. A reporter later wrote that the crater's "interior was churned up, as though by a giant egg beater." Another compared the crater to a scene from a science-fiction film.

Dr. Ken Gobel treated First Lieutenant Farnham and the other survivor, Maj. Wilbur F. Minnich of Illinois. The men were not seriously hurt, but both were suffering from shock. Once he was certain the injuries were not life-threatening, Dr. Gobel asked an important question: "Did you guys have 'a big one' aboard?" They assured him that there were no nuclear weapons on the plane. Gobel persisted. "Now you level with me," he said. "I'm the doctor in this area and I've got to take care of these people!"

Not long after Trooper Kirkman arrived at the scene, helicopters equipped with spotlights scanned the area for possible survivors and parts of the B-52. Soldiers from Seymour Johnson Air Force Base, Civil Air Patrol, Civil Defense, and Salvation Army workers aided in the search. By 3 A.M. hundreds of people had gathered next to John Frank's field. Cars clogged the dirt road leading to his home. Halted by police, many curiosity seekers walked 3 or 4 miles to view the wreckage. At one point a few rounds of ammunition exploded, driving the crowd back to the field's far edge.

The bodies of six crewmen were recovered. Only Farnham and Minnich survived the crash. The cause was never determined. There were no nuclear weapons aboard. The wreckage was gradually removed and the crater filled in.

In March 2003, forty-two years after the Denton crash, about 300 people gathered at Camp Walter Johnson for a memorial service for those who died. Lowe Garner of Denton had been researching the incident for a year and had decided he wanted to honor the crew of the fallen bomber. Present at the service were former patrolman Kirkman, who had become mayor of Denton; Glen Farnham, who had retired from the Air Force in 1978 as a lieutenant colonel; and family members of several of the victims. Farnham thanked the people of Denton for the help and hospitality they provided during the incident.

Retrieval of the rest of the nuclear device buried near Goldsboro was permanently discontinued when the cost became prohibitive. The Air Force covered the hole and purchased an easement from Charles T. Davis, owner of the property, and his heirs. The conveyance document prohibits "drilling, digging, boring, excavating or other disturbances of the land . . . below a depth of five (5) feet." Use of the land was limited to "the growing of crops, the growing of timber, or as pasture."

Most experts eventually agreed that neither of the weapons could have detonated unless the aircraft commander threw the arming switch located in the cockpit. The consensus was that it was virtually impossible for that switch to be activated accidentally. Similar accidents in other parts of the country prompted the Kennedy administration to reduce SAC airborne alert activity and order more elaborate safety mechanisms installed on nuclear weapons.

As a more complex pattern of international politics developed during the 1960s and 1970s, relations between the United States and the Soviet Union began to thaw. Agreements signed by both nations in 1972 and 1979 set limits on antiballistic missiles and on strategic missiles capable of carrying nuclear weapons. Tensions increased again in the early 1980s, but in 1991 the Soviet Union collapsed. Fifteen newly independent nations emerged, including Russia, whose democratic election of an anticommunist leader drove a final nail into the Cold War's coffin.

At the writing of this book, the North Carolina Division of Radiation Protection still periodically tests groundwater near the Goldsboro crash site. A spokesman interviewed in 2001 said that nothing of concern had been discovered to date.

CHAPTER 16

Terrain! Terrain!

THE CRASH OF FLIGHT 1016

— 1994 —

AT 6:28 P.M. ON JULY 2, 1994, CAPTAIN MICHAEL
Greenlee made an announcement: "Ladies and gentlemen, we're 40
miles from Charlotte. . . . At this time we'd like our flight attendants
to please prepare the cabin for arrival."

Richard DeMary, Shelley Markwith, and Karen Forcht—the
three flight attendants aboard US Air Flight 1016—checked to make
sure seat belts were fastened, tray tables were upright and locked,

*When Flight 1016 fell from the sky on July 2, 1994, it broke apart into three big
sections. The aft cabin and tail section came to rest against a carport on Wallace
Neel Road.* Diedra Laird/*Charlotte Observer*

carry-on bags were stowed under seats, the seats themselves were upright, and overhead bins were closed securely.

It had been a short twenty-minute flight from Columbia, South Carolina, to Charlotte, North Carolina. The attendants had barely had time to serve beverages. DeMary and Markwith settled into jumpseats at the front of the DC-9 jet, with their backs against the cockpit wall. Attendant Forcht sat in a jumpseat at the other end. In the last row was a young woman with a nine-month-old baby. Forcht peeked around the corner a few times, making the baby laugh.

Based on information received on takeoff from Columbia, Captain Greenlee expected the weather in Charlotte to be partly cloudy with a temperature around ninety degrees. As Flight 1016 drew closer to the airport, however, Greenlee saw what appeared to be a thunderstorm.

"There's more rain than I thought there was," said First Officer James Hayes, who was flying the plane.

Greenlee, age thirty-eight, and Hayes, forty-one, were both seasoned pilots. Concerned about the shifting weather, the two men listened closely to their radio. Aircraft just ahead of them were reporting smooth landings, but rain was hammering the DC-9's windshield. Greenlee flipped a switch, turning on the wipers. The plane was now about 2 miles from the runway.

A voice from the Charlotte tower broke in: "Wind shear alert. Northeast boundary. Winds one nine zero at one three." Not long after that, the tower addressed US Air Flight 806, awaiting departure: "806, looks like we've gotten a storm right on top of the field here." Flight 806 and TWA Flight 797, also on the ground, both notified the tower that they would wait until the weather cleared.

Troubled by the wind, rain, and poor visibility, Greenlee told Hayes to circle around for another attempt. Hayes added power and turned to the right. Flight attendant DeMary felt the aircraft tilt upward. Then, instead of continuing in that direction as he expected it to, the plane suddenly sank. He cast a worried glance at Markwith.

They both tightened their seat belts. DeMary assumed the brace position: feet flat on the floor, hands tucked under his legs. He sat straight up with the back of his head against the padding on the back of his jumpseat.

One of the passengers, a military air traffic controller, could tell the pilot was having serious trouble. Others knew only what their senses told them. Without warning, the jet plunged into the middle of a dark rain cloud. The engine slowed down, then sped up. Rain struck the wing at a slant. The plane bounced, jolted, and bumped like a roller coaster—and then it dropped.

The woman whose baby had laughed at attendant Forcht clutched the infant, her eyes wide with terror. Two rows in front of her, a woman traveling with her nineteen-month-old daughter leaned forward and pulled the toddler toward her, grasping her tightly with both arms.

DeMary, seated against the cockpit wall, heard the Ground Proximity Warning System's *whoop-whoop* sound. A mechanical voice intoned: "Terrain. Terrain."

We're going down, DeMary thought. *We're crashing.*

The plane shook violently. Passengers felt jolt after jolt as they were thrown up, back, over, and back again. Flames blew up in their faces, singeing hair and skin. The woman holding the nine-month-old baby screamed as the infant flew out of her arms.

Later DeMary remembered only two impacts, the first with the ground. He heard metal screeching and what sounded like trees breaking, followed by a second, even more brutal hit. The plane came to a stop. Rain pelted DeMary; a gust of wind slapped his face. He was aware that he had jet fuel on him. He grabbed the handle of the nearby exit door, but it would not turn. At almost the same moment, he realized that he did not need to open a door. The cabin was gone. All he could see were a few rows of seats. He sat at an angle, leaning against attendant Markwith.

"I need help," Markwith said. "I can't get out."

July 2, 1994, had started quietly for Richard DeMary. Designated lead flight attendant for US Air Flight 1016, he had arrived at Pittsburgh International Airport in the morning and held a briefing with Markwith and Forcht. They discussed emergency procedures for the Douglas DC-9 jet they were about to board as well as how they would organize food and drink service. Captain Greenlee also briefed the crew, encouraging the attendants to come to the cockpit and speak with him if they encountered problems during the flight.

Just before takeoff, DeMary fastened his shoulder harness and mentally reviewed critical issues: What is my emergency exit? What do I do if my exit is blocked? Which way does the handle rotate? What are my actions at the usable exits? What is my command or what is my brace signal? What is the brace position? He also took note of environmental conditions. That morning the weather in Pittsburgh was pleasant—partly cloudy, with a temperature of about eighty degrees. A gentle breeze was blowing. Nothing to worry about there. He noted that New York was about the same.

At age thirty-two, DeMary had been a flight attendant for two years. For four years before that, he had worked as an airline customer service agent. Airplanes had fascinated him for as long as he could remember—in his words, he was "always watching them and listening for them and imagining being up there." He had a private pilot's license and about 120 hours of experience at the controls. Being a flight attendant had never been DeMary's life ambition, but he enjoyed his work.

On July 2 US Air 1016's flight sequence included a trip from Pittsburgh to New York and from there to Charlotte, North Carolina, and Columbia, South Carolina. The crew would then make a return trip to Charlotte and finish in Memphis, Tennessee. Fifty-two passengers boarded Flight 1016 in Columbia, filling about half the seats on the plane. For the fourth time that day, DeMary pointed out emergency exits and demonstrated the use of seat belts, oxygen masks, and flotation devices.

In seat 19D, Christine Peters, a business professional in her mid-forties, turned to the man next to her. She joked about being in the "crash and burn seats," and the two of them discussed the location of the fuel tanks. "Oh well," Peters said, "it's Fourth of July weekend. We'll make good fireworks."

At 6:15 P.M. Captain Greenlee spoke to the passengers over the public address system: "Good afternoon, folks, from the flight deck. We'd like to say welcome aboard to you. We'll be on our way momentarily to Charlotte. . . . The weather up there is just about what you see out the window . . . partly cloudy skies . . . they have ninety degrees on the last hour."

Once the flight was under way, Greenlee and Hayes chatted about the various type of planes they had flown. In the cabin the flight attendants served beverages. A toddler in a pink tank top and shorts seemed especially pleased that they had lemonade.

Not long after the attendants collected the cups and took their seats, the plane began to bump and jolt. Most of the passengers thought they were experiencing an unusual amount of turbulence but nothing worse. Then, the jet suddenly dropped.

Witnesses on the ground later said they saw Flight 1016 emerge from the rain and clouds about one-quarter of a mile from the end of the runway. The downpour was intense; the wind was blowing hard. The jet seemed to disappear in a wall of water. It hit the ground in a field next to the runway, and crashed into a wooded area, shearing off trees. Then it broke apart into three big sections.

A minister who lived near the airport was watching the lightning and rain. To his horror, he saw the DC-9 dive to earth, landing about 200 yards from where he sat. A woman driving along Wallace Neel Road slammed on her brakes as the plane's tail skidded in front of her in flames. She struggled to control her car as it went into a spin and came to a stop only after becoming entangled in fallen telephone wires. She was not hurt, but she later found an airline-size liquor bottle lodged in the front grill of her car.

The calls to the 911 emergency notification system began at 6:43 P.M. A young woman reported the crash, then an older woman. Next came a call from a woman on her car phone. "Is it a little airplane or is it one with a lot of windows?" asked the dispatcher. "It's blown up," said the caller. "It's not together."

About a mile from the crash, John Roberts and his family were outside their house, gathering up building materials in anticipation of the thunderstorm. His wife later recalled hearing what sounded like "a train coming toward us." The thirty-eight-year-old maintenance worker jumped into his truck and drove toward the smoke.

In the deformed nose of the plane, Richard DeMary came to his senses enough to realize that he needed to evacuate people. He began to yell: "Release seat belts and get out! Release seat belts and get out!" Next to him, Shelley Markwith shouted the same commands. DeMary unbuckled Markwith's seat belt for her. He noticed she was burned and her leg was so badly hurt that she could not stand up. DeMary grabbed her in a "bear hug," lifted her, and stepped into Wallace Neel Road.

At the other end of the jet, the woman with the toddler drifted in and out of consciousness. She pulled her child out of the rubble by her leg. There was blood on her face, but she was alive. Two rows behind her, a woman moaned, "Where is my baby? I can't find my baby!"

The man in seat 19F near the rear of the DC-9 awoke under a pile of metal. He could barely breathe because of the weight on his chest. Not far from him Christine Peters could breathe fine but dared not— for fear of inhaling too much smoke. Covered with tree branches and plane debris, she ordered herself not to panic and focused on getting out. When she saw flight attendant Forcht crawling over the wreckage, she asked how she could help.

Forcht and Peters tried to open the back rear emergency door. It seemed like a losing proposition. The floor was bent so that it partially blocked the exit. Nevertheless, they were able to force the door open a crack. All they could see were flames.

Small fires burned everywhere. As DeMary struggled to get Markwith to safety, he suddenly realized they were in a residential area. He saw houses, trees, and sidewalks. The plane's tail section had lodged in the carport of someone's home. He found a shed in the backyard where he felt Markwith would be safe.

Disoriented and in shock, DeMary took off his tie and wandered toward the tail section, where everything was eerily quiet. He heard no one, saw no one. For a moment he wondered if only he and Markwith had survived the crash. The thought was unbearable. He began to walk beside the aircraft yelling the command: "Release seat belts and get out!" It was a starting point, he decided, something that might get people moving.

Passenger Christine Peters returned to where her seat had been. Glancing to her left, she noticed something beyond strange: a door leading into a kitchen. Confused, she tried the door but could not open it. The glass pane was not broken and she could not find anything with which to break it.

DeMary felt a surge of hope when a young woman appeared in the break in the fuselage. He helped her to the shed where he had taken Markwith. Returning to the plane, he continued to shout his command.

Minutes after leaving home, John Roberts found himself at a horrific scene: great hunks of sheared metal surrounded by flames and smoke. People wandered aimlessly, dazed and half blind. A woman staggered toward him, soaked with jet fuel, crying that she had lost her child. Both her arms were broken. Roberts fashioned a sling from his shirt and slipped her arms into it. Fearing that the plane might explode at any moment, he walked her to a fence behind a nearby house and lifted her over it into the hands of neighborhood residents.

Sherrie Hudson was on her way home when she came upon the crash scene. She got out of her car and hurried down Wallace Neel Road, appalled by the screams, black smoke, and the stench of jet fuel and charred flesh. Among the wandering wounded she noticed an adolescent boy stumbling along by himself. She immediately went to comfort him. He seemed to be having trouble breathing. After a moment, he pointed to a bronchial inhaler in his pocket, and Hudson helped him use it to relieve his asthma. There was nothing she could do about the second- and third-degree burns on his back, arms, and legs.

Emergency crews began to arrive. The Charlotte tower had activated the "crash phone" at 6:45 P.M. Firefighters responded with aircraft rescue and firefighting trucks. A quick-response-and-command truck joined them. They quickly extinguished all fires and started searching for trapped and injured people. Paramedics and ambulances from surrounding communities were also on the scene.

"It got so hot," one fireman later recalled, "we could spend only minutes aiming the foam lines at the flames before nearly collapsing."

Flight attendant Forcht made her way out of the wreckage with several other passengers, including Christine Peters. They dropped about 8 feet and landed on the front porch of the house that was connected to the demolished carport. All of them were severely burned—not just from the crash but from touching hot metal as they shimmied out of the airplane. The homeowners were not there. They had gone away for the Fourth of July holiday weekend.

Under the wreckage in the carport, DeMary found an injured, semiconscious passenger still in his seat belt. He helped rescue workers move fallen telephone poles so that their trucks could get closer. The man was saved. An ambulance carried the boy comforted by Sherrie Hudson to the hospital. Hudson visited and telephoned him several times during his recovery.

Although dazed and disoriented, Captain Greenlee and First Officer Hayes refused treatment, telling rescue workers to take care of other victims first. Greenlee took on the job of pouring saline water over attendant Forcht's burns. DeMary finally had time to assess his own injuries. The nerves in one foot had been severed, his leg was swelling, and he had burns on his arm. Captain Greenlee and First Officer Hayes both suffered cuts and bruises. Hayes broke his left foot.

Of the flight's fifty-seven occupants (fifty-two passengers and five crew members), twenty survived. Among the dead were the baby whose mother had not been able to hold onto her during the crash, a couple who had just been married that afternoon, and a family of five on their way to New York to visit relatives.

The crew underwent drug testing. Nothing was found. The National Transportation Safety Board listed four probable causes for the crash, "all of which led to an encounter with and failure to escape from a microburst-induced windshear that was produced by a rapidly developing thunderstorm located at the approach end of runway 18R." Windshear is an abrupt shift in wind speed and direction. Four contributing factors were also listed. Responsibility was spread among the flight crew, air traffic control, and inadequate software logic in the airplane's windshear warning system.

For his courageous actions during the disaster, Richard DeMary was given the Flight Safety Foundation's Heroism Award for 1994 as well as numerous other recognitions.

The city of Charlotte bought a new home for the people whose house had been irreparably damaged in the crash.

In 1996 a memorial ceremony was held for the families of the victims, and a 2½-foot stone marker was unveiled near the airport. It reads: IN LOVING MEMORY OF ALL THOSE WHO DIED OR WERE INJURED AND THOSE WHO HELPED IN THE RESCUE AND RESTORATION OF US AIR #1016, JULY 2, 1994.

CHAPTER 17

A Risky Business

THE SPEEDWAY DISASTER
— *2000* —

FROM THE VERY BEGINNING, IT WAS SPEED THAT
attracted the crowd—speed, the roar of the engines, the splatter of
dirt, and the smell of rubber and fuel. Back in 1949, when stock car
racing got its start, spectators gathered to watch drivers zoom around
a track, not in fancy race cars but in automobiles like those the average person drove every day. Of course, the average person usually did
not accelerate to 80 miles per hour and above.

On Sunday, June 19, 1949, about 20,000 fans showed up at the
fairgrounds in Charlotte, North Carolina. They caused traffic jams

*A wrecking crew tore down the end of the walkway left standing after the bridge
collapsed in May 2000. "We were just walking across," a witness recalled. "Then it
just went down."* Photo courtesy D.H. Griffin Wrecking Co.

and filled every available seat around the track. The air was alive with anticipation, infused with a touch of anxiety. Racing was dangerous business. There was always a chance that something might go horribly wrong. Most fans did not want that to happen, but they knew it could.

The flag dropped. Engines rumbled; wheels spun. A Chrysler took the turns on the banked track at 50 miles per hour, then hit 90 on the straightaway. A Hudson flew into the corner sideways, spewing dirt in every direction. The crowd, mostly men and boys, shouted and cheered, waved their hats, and slapped each other on the back. A Buick flipped four times before coming to a stop. The driver crawled out and sat at the edge of the track, his head in his hands. He was not badly hurt, but he had no way to get home. Worse, he had no idea how he was going to explain a crumpled mass of metal to the man who had loaned him the Buick.

After the dust cleared, Glenn Dunnaway was declared the winner of the first true NASCAR race. He was then disqualified for using an illegal "wedge" to increase his speed. Second-place driver Jim Roper of Kansas was awarded the trophy. The race was over, but a new era in automobile racing was just beginning.

Eleven years later, people were still flocking to Charlotte—or rather to Concord, just northeast of the city. On June 19, 1960, the new 40,000-seat Charlotte Motor Speedway hosted the first World 600 race. The combination of prowess and peril was as attractive as ever to the 36,000 fans. They sat on the edge of their seats, watching Fireball Roberts, Junior Johnson, and Richard Petty zoom by at more than 150 miles per hour. Cars blew tires and spun off the track. At least one caught fire. A few crashed into guardrails. A flying hunk of fresh asphalt ruptured a gas tank.

Over the next fifty years, the world of NASCAR changed tremendously. Spectators who attended the Winston in Concord in 2000 numbered 120,000 instead of the usual 20,000 or 36,000 who attended in the 1950s and 1960s. The crowd was different in other ways as well. In the earlier days women simply were not invited to races, and that was fine with most of them. As one newspaper columnist recalled: "My mom was horrified by it . . . sunburnt men walking around with no shirts, sweating and drinking all day." In contrast, by 2000, more than one-third of NASCAR's fans were female. Writer Joe Menzer described the throng that assembled on May 20: "There are plenty of beer-guzzling rednecks, to be sure; but there are also lawyers and doctors, accountants and insurance adjusters—college graduates all."

Renamed Lowe's Motor Speedway in 1995, the Concord track complex contained a seven-story building with offices, shops, and dining facilities. Condominiums towered over the first turn. The grandstand accommodated 167,000 people, and there was room for 50,000 more in the infield area. As always speed, intense competition, and unpredictability attracted crowds. Qualifying speeds—under 100 miles per hour in 1949—were now in the neighborhood of 180 miles per hour. NASCAR had added numerous safety measures to protect its drivers, but a tantalizing undercurrent of risk remained. In fact, some would argue, the risk was even greater because drivers were likely to take more chances, counting on the added safeguards to preserve them.

On Saturday night, May 20, campers and recreational vehicles filled designated areas of the infield. People had begun to gather the day before to watch practices and qualifying runs. Almost everyone wore a jacket, T-shirt, or hat bearing the name of a NASCAR hero: Earnhardt, Jarrett, Martin, Labonte, Wallace, Elliott. The aroma of grilled hamburgers and chicken flavored the air. The sheer size of the speedway complex seemed to confirm that the Winston was indeed a "big deal." Sometimes described as stock car racing's version of an all-star game, the race was part of Speed Week, a series of events culminating in the Coca-Cola 600.

As the time approached for the start of the Winston, hundreds of fans surged onto two steel-and-concrete walkways that connected the parking lot to the speedway. The 16-foot-wide pedestrian bridges had been built so that people would not have to cross a four-lane highway to get to and from the races.

The weather was dry and pleasant that evening. A former school-teacher from Charleston, West Virginia, walked over the bridge with his wife, son, and seven-year-old granddaughter. A married couple in their thirties from Rockwell, North Carolina, strolled across, laughing at a private joke. A man from Huntersville, north of Charlotte, escorted his eighty-three-year-old grandmother. A young South Carolina man in a Mark Martin T-shirt argued good-naturedly with his father-in-law, a Dale Earnhardt Jr. fan.

The sights, sounds, and smells of racing had drawn them all to Concord. Lugging coolers and seat cushions, they poured into the grandstand. Excitement intensified throughout the crowd of 180,000 as brightly painted Fords, Chevrolets, and Pontiacs pulled into position on the track. The race was divided into three segments consisting of thirty laps, thirty laps, and ten laps. Teams would have a ten-minute break between segments. The winner would have to successfully complete seventy laps around the 1.5-mile track and finish ahead of everyone else.

Fans removed their hats and placed hand over heart as country music star Lorrie Morgan sang the national anthem. Next came the four most familiar words in racing: "Gentlemen, start your engines!" Motors growled and grumbled to life. The crowd, most of them already on their feet, cheered, whistled, and shouted. A NASCAR official dropped the green flag. The pack buzzed around the track, sounding like a swarm of giant hornets. The grandstands seemed to come alive beneath the spectators' feet each time they passed.

During the second segment of the race, the car driven by Jeff Gordon spun in a turn. Driver Steve Park slowed down to avoid a collision, which caused a three-car crash. All three drivers were able to get repairs and return to the track. Then, with eight laps left in the last segment, cars driven by Joe Nemechek and Steve Park banged into each other coming out of turn two. In turn three they collided violently. People in the stands gasped in horror as the cars spun into the path of two other drivers, who could not avoid slamming into them. An official waved a yellow flag, indicating a hazard on the track. Tension gripped the spectators until it was clear that all four drivers were safe.

Eight laps later, an official waved the checkered flag as Dale Earnhardt Jr. completed lap seventy ahead of the pack. The race had lasted close to forty minutes. It had been exactly the kind most fans liked to see: plenty of thrills and no serious injuries or fatalities.

People talked animatedly as they exited the speedway and climbed the ramp to the bridge that spanned Highway 29. It was after 11 P.M. Small children slept in their parents' arms. The man in the Mark Martin T-shirt shook his head, bewildered, as his father-in-law, the Earnhardt Jr. fan, chuckled. Martin had come in seventeenth. The husband and wife from Rockwell chatted excitedly. She had won $100 in a company pool. Tired, happy fans shuffled en masse across the walkway, the penetrating drone of the race still resonating in their ears. They had no reason to believe they were in any danger.

At about 11:15 P.M. the former schoolteacher from West Virginia was partway across the bridge with his family when he heard a loud crack, followed by a second crack. A New Yorker standing beside one of the walkways heard what sounded to him like an explosion. He thought it might be fireworks going off in Victory Lane. A man from Columbia, South Carolina, who was just stepping off the bridge thought the same thing. He turned to make a comment to his friend. What he saw rendered him speechless.

"The bridge is collapsing!" someone yelled.

On May 20, 2000, a pedestrian bridge at Lowe's Motor Speedway "fell out from under" fans who had come to watch The Winston. Nearly ninety people were transported from the scene to area hospitals for treatment of injuries. Charlotte Observer *file photo*

Suddenly the West Virginia schoolteacher felt nothing beneath his feet. He jerked his granddaughter into the air as he fell. The eighty-three-year-old woman from Huntersville and her thirty-six-year-old grandson stared in horror as the pavement about a foot in front of them disappeared. The grandson quickly snapped several pictures with his compact camera. His grandmother tugged at him and he realized he had to get her off the bridge.

To some it felt like an earthquake. People near the break in the walkway grabbed onto a fence to keep from falling, cutting their hands and wrenching their fingers in the process. Screaming in terror, adults and children slid and rolled down the concrete slope. Others plunged more than 15 feet, free falling to the ground. They tumbled onto each other and onto a pile of jagged rock. Many were hit by chunks of falling cement. The former schoolteacher landed hard, wrenching his ankle and scraping his elbow. His granddaughter landed on his stomach.

"We were just walking across," a witness recalled. "Then it just went down. Everybody was on top of each other. It was awful. I figured somebody was going to get killed in it."

The South Carolina man who had just stepped off the bridge before it collapsed shouted his friend's name. He received no reply. Frantic, he dashed down to the street to look for him. People were running everywhere, hollering and crying. He spotted his friend trapped in the rubble, sitting up, dazed. He called his name again. The friend did not seem to hear him.

Mercifully, Highway 29 was closed to traffic because of the race. It also happened that emergency response teams assigned to cover the race were still on hand. A paramedic about 200 yards away saw the walkway sag, then collapse, forming a V shape in the middle of the road. He and his ambulance crew maneuvered through panicked crowds, arriving at the scene in seconds. The call went out to Mecklenburg County's emergency medical service (Medic). Squads were dispatched from Gaston, Iredell, Union, Stanly, and Rowan Counties.

Before rescuers could even begin to get people out, they first had to cut through the fencing that surrounded the bridge. Victims were piled three and four deep. Coolers, souvenirs, and other personal belongings were scattered about. Everywhere paramedics turned they saw gaping wounds and bones protruding from legs and arms. People stepped out of the crowd, identifying themselves as nurses or doctors, asking what they could do to help.

Immediately two triage centers were set up. After people were removed from the debris, they were evaluated and assigned a colored tag—red for the most seriously injured, yellow for those whose condition was urgent but for whom treatment could be delayed up to one hour, and green for those who could wait up to three hours. Area hospitals called in surgeons and additional staff in anticipation of the large number of casualties.

The man in the Mark Martin T-shirt was assigned a yellow tag and transported to NorthEast Medical Center. His right knee ached, but he was mostly concerned about losing his lower left leg. His foot and ankle had been shattered into several pieces. A nurse rolled his stretcher around to one side of the unit. Near him other adults and children waited for painkillers and surgery. Later he learned that his father-in-law had been found hanging from a fence, his lower back fractured, ribs bruised, and shoulder injured. Medics had reached him within four minutes of the accident, and he had also been taken to NorthEast.

"Having ten seriously injured people in an emergency department at one time defines a disaster," a trauma nurse coordinator at North-East told a reporter. That night her hospital received nearly fifty victims within a ninety-minute period. The surgical staff worked six operating rooms at once.

The married couple from Rockwell sustained multiple injuries: She suffered a broken arm and vertebra; he broke four bones in his left foot and leg. Screws were required to reattach two leg bones to an ankle. The Mark Martin fan required two surgeries, but his leg was saved.

In all, nearly ninety people were transported from the scene in less than an hour. Some spent four to five hours in surgery. Others were treated for minor injuries and released. There were no deaths.

"The nature of the accident dictated that it should have been much worse," said the manager of the emergency department at Rowan Regional Medical Center. "Those people were very lucky." Victims and rescuers agreed that the quick response of emergency teams and the planning and dedication of hospital staff and physicians were part of that "luck."

On Sunday, May 21, track president H. A. "Humpy" Wheeler appeared at a news conference. "Our prayers, our thoughts, our sympathies go out to the injured and their families," he said. The ruined walkway section was moved to another site at the speedway for examination. Concern about a second pedestrian bridge 500 yards from the first prompted officials to close that bridge until the reasons for the collapse could be analyzed.

A week later, on May 28, a crowd of 200,000 converged on the speedway for the Coca-Cola 600. They used the two ground-level crosswalks on Highway 29 in an orderly fashion, as they had before the pedestrian bridges were built. Police stopped traffic periodically and escorted waves of visitors across the four-lane road.

Engineers eventually determined that the bridge failed because steel support cables that ran through it had rusted, due to the use of a grout mixture containing calcium chloride. The mixture was used to plug holes at the center of the walkway. Calcium chloride speeds the hardening of concrete but also retains moisture, permitting rust to form more easily. Examination of the second walkway revealed that calcium chloride was not used in its construction. By October 2000 the defective pedestrian bridge had been rebuilt.

For the most severely injured victims, the road to recovery was to be long and agonizing. Lawsuits were filed against the speedway, the construction company, and the company that made the grout. In March 2003 one couple was awarded a $4 million settlement.

Automobile racing is known as a risky business, yet that does not deter drivers or fans from enjoying the sport. Following the walkway collapse, people interviewed by reporters commented that taking chances is part of life. "Accidents can happen anywhere," said one woman. "We all take risks every day," replied another.

As for Jim Roper, winner of that first "strictly stock car" race in Charlotte, he quit racing in 1955 after breaking a vertebrae. In 1999 the Atlanta Motor Speedway honored him for being the first person to win in the Grand National Division, which became the NASCAR Winston Cup Series. Roper, who had been ill with cancer and suffered from heart and liver failure, passed away June 23, 2000—a month after the walkway at Lowe's Motor Speedway collapsed. He was eighty-three.

CHAPTER 18

White Wedding, Black Ice

THE FEBRUARY SNOWSTORM

— 2004 —

AS FEBRUARY 2004 DREW TO A CLOSE, CHARLOTTE looked forward to entertaining an important guest: President George W. Bush was coming to visit on Thursday, February 26. Other meaningful events were also scheduled, occurrences important to a fairly small group of people but significant nonetheless. One was the wedding of Anne Baltz and Ryan Kelley on Saturday, February 28. Friends and relatives were coming from as far north as Minnesota and as far south as Texas to share in the celebration.

Charlotte residents were skeptical when a winter storm was predicted for February 26, 2004. Within twenty-four hours, nearly a foot of snow had accumulated. The next night, falling temperatures turned snow, puddles, and slush to ice, making even plowed roads treacherous. Gary O'Brien/Charlotte Observer

Charlotte always liked to dress up for special occasions, and this time she decided to wear white. If she had been a woman, this might not have created much of a stir. However, Charlotte is a city—a Southern city—and the fabric of her white outfit was guaranteed to cause alarm.

Newspapers were among the first to deliver the warning: "A winter storm may dump as much as 5 inches of wet, heavy snow on Charlotte," declared the *Charlotte Observer*. Quite a few residents responded with a big shrug. They had weathered three false alarms in the past month. "We don't get excited anymore when the weatherman tells us to," said a police department dispatcher. "Meteorologists, they all lie," said one highway patrol officer with a grin.

The Air Force and Secret Service kept an eye on things for President Bush but did not anticipate any problems. Up in Minneapolis, Milwaukee, and Chicago, wedding guests continued with their travel plans. The weather was pretty nice where they were, and they were heading south. How bad could it be?

At midnight on Wednesday, February 25, *Charlotte Observer* reporter Dan Huntley went outside to feed his dogs. "There was little wind and it wasn't that cold," he commented later. "I wasn't even wearing shoes. I thought to myself, *Rain maybe. But no way we're gonna have any white stuff.*"

Huntley and the rest of Charlotte awoke on Thursday morning to the sight of swirling white flakes falling on already white lawns. Huntley shuddered as he remembered the words of the television weatherman the night before: "A massive front of moisture is heading our way. . . ." But his wife, a schoolteacher, said school had not been canceled. That usually meant conditions were not expected to get very bad. "Like many others, my wife, daughter and I trudged off to work," Huntley wrote.

Anne Baltz, who was staying at her mother's home in Charlotte, got out early and went to a copy shop to have wedding programs printed. Thursday afternoon, she and her mother tried to go out again. Ice and snow caused the car to run off the road. Fortunately Anne's younger brother was onboard. He and the bride-to-be pushed the car out of a ditch. Anne tried not to worry about her grandparents, aunt, and uncle who were flying down from Wisconsin. Meanwhile, high in the air, Anne's relatives were being told their plane could not land in Charlotte because of the weather conditions. They would be diverted to Columbia, South Carolina.

Three hours after Dan Huntley arrived at work, he was back on the road, slipping and sliding toward home. Schools, banks, doctors' offices, malls, and some grocery stores closed early. Traffic backed up all over town. One reporter described the exodus from downtown Charlotte as "the largest midday evacuation since the September 11, 2001, terrorist attacks." The snow kept falling. To the relief of local law enforcement officials, President Bush canceled his visit. Police and emergency medical personnel already had their hands full responding to hundreds of crashes.

Anne's fiancé, Ryan, made it safely to Charlotte from Asheville. He too was concerned about traveling family members, some driving from Minnesota or Texas, others flying in from Mississippi. The plane carrying his mother and her husband arrived from Chicago just before the Charlotte airport shut down. The couple rented a car and headed for their hotel, expecting about a twenty-minute drive. Before long they realized how far off that estimate was likely to be. Roads were snow covered and treacherous. A combination of bad weather, nervous drivers, and short tempers created havoc. Major accidents shut down highways all across the area. The 18-mile trip from airport to hotel took an hour and a half.

According to media reports, between 8:00 A.M. and 3:30 P.M. Mecklenburg County's 911 emergency notification system (Medic) received 105 calls from cell phones (compared with 15 the day before). Medic responded to nearly seventy crashes with potential injuries.

Callers did not always know the exact location of the wrecks, which complicated matters. About five people called for each accident on the road, and most of them did not know whether anyone was injured. An ambulance had to be dispatched just in case.

A center answering after-hours calls for doctors took more than 31,000 calls on Thursday—nearly six times the normal volume.

At midnight, Ryan's bachelor party was in full swing. His closest friends had made it to town from various places in the Carolinas. They were having a good time, in spite of the fact that they were stuck in Ryan's hotel room.

Outside, Mecklenburg County EMTs were not having any fun at all. By midnight six ambulances were stuck in the snow. Paramedics had to get out and walk, often carrying heavy equipment, in order to reach sick or injured people. A woman went into labor in south Charlotte and called 911. She was relayed in a volunteer firefighter's car to a Medic supervisor's truck, which took her to the hospital. This "leap-frogging" approach was used repeatedly throughout the storm.

At Charlotte-Douglas International Airport, airline employees de-iced planes until 4 A.M., when the last scheduled Thursday flight took off. Three dozen flights had been canceled.

Between Thursday morning and Friday morning, Medic received around 350 calls for help compared to about 180 calls during the same period the day before. Medical emergency crews were sent to eighty-six traffic accidents—four times the usual number. It wasn't that residents of the Charlotte area had never seen snow before. Just a month earlier, the city had been hard hit by a winter storm that caused widespread power outages and traffic fatalities. Three things set this February storm apart: the amount of snow (11.6 inches, as it turned out), the short time in which the snow accumulated (twenty-four hours), and the fact that most of the snow fell in the middle of the day rather than overnight, when most people would have been at home.

Hoping to provide comic relief, the February 27 *Charlotte Observer* offered a poem by staff writer Tommy Tomlinson. It was a parody of the Dr. Seuss classic *And to Think That I Saw It on Mulberry Street.* The poem began:

> What a wild day it was here in old Caroline.
> Snow up to your belly and over your spine.
> Plus a wind that was so cold it froze your behine,
> And to think that we saw it in old Caroline!

Road crews spent the night plowing, scraping, and salting. By Friday morning 15 inches of snow had fallen in parts of Charlotte, with up to 18 inches in surrounding areas.

While some of the city's inhabitants made the most of the opportunity to go sledding or build a snowman, others found the situation unpleasant, even frightening. Friday morning a call came in to Medic on the nonemergency line. A seventy-five-year-old diabetic woman had run out of syringes for her daily doses of insulin. Normally, a home health nurse was on hand to help the woman, but snow had prevented the nurse from coming by.

Medic worker Mike Stanford was about ready to go home. His usual job was scheduling, but he had been up more than twenty-four hours answering emergency telephone calls and picking up stranded coworkers. Medic workers did not typically deliver supplies, but Stanford volunteered to take the syringes to the woman. When he arrived, he found that he had the wrong syringes. He drove to a pharmacy and bought more. The woman, who was losing her sight, had trouble seeing the lines for proper doses, so Stanford helped fill the syringes for her.

At Charlotte-Douglas International Airport, hundreds of travelers waited in line, many of whom had been stranded overnight.

Hotels had filled up quickly, and people not fortunate enough to get a room had spent the night on airport cots.

Sport-utility vehicle drivers made themselves useful. One high school student drove through town Thursday night and all day Friday looking for snowbound cars. He freed his neighbors' automobiles, then helped fifteen strangers, including a mailman. A physician used his SUV to nudge a police car and four other sliding vehicles up a hill.

An SUV came to the rescue of Anne Baltz as well. Her maid of honor drove her around on Friday in one—to the airport and various locations in town to pick up bridesmaids, to the bakery for the rehearsal dinner cake, and to the florist. The flower truck was stuck on a highway off-ramp for five or six hours, causing late delivery. Then came a call from the caterer: The wedding could not be held at the planned location in Fort Mill, South Carolina (about 20 miles south of Charlotte). The entrance road and parking lot were under a foot and a half of snow and could not possibly be plowed in time.

Another inch of snow fell Friday afternoon. City and state road crews, running short of rock salt, went to work yet again and stayed on the job for the second straight night. Temperatures fell into the twenties. Snow, puddles, and slush froze, making even plowed roads treacherous. Around 9 o'clock, the number of accidents rose sharply. Even tow trucks were getting stuck.

Fortunately for Anne and Ryan, the caterer who delivered the bad news about the wedding location had a solution. A country club not far from the original wedding site was available. Anne would have to notify the guests, the disc jockey, and the photographer of the change. There could be no rehearsal, but the manager and staff of a Charlotte restaurant made sure the rehearsal dinner was held as planned. Everyone who had been invited was there, including Anne's Wisconsin relatives, who had traveled by bus from Columbia.

Reporter-turned-poet Tomlinson tipped his hat to weather forecasters (with apologies to Dr. Seuss):

The meteorologists shimmied with glee.

"We told you!" they said. "It was gonna snow. See?"

(Which brings up their average to one out of three).

And to think that we saw it on weather TV!

As snow cascaded off roofs and awnings, burglar alarms were activated, requiring police to investigate.

Early Saturday morning, sheets of black ice formed on roads, causing dozens of accidents. Many SUV drivers discovered that four-wheel drive did not really help much on ice. Often overconfident and occasionally foolhardy, they landed in ditches and snowdrifts and had to be pulled out. At 3 A.M., Medic workers on their way home spotted an overturned SUV on an interstate highway ramp. Joined by two passersby, they checked to make sure the passengers were okay. They had just called for help when they noticed a car speeding toward them out of control.

A Medic employee pushed one of the passersby out of the way, slipped on the icy ground, and fell. The oncoming car missed them but slammed into a guardrail. No one was severely hurt, but the Medic worker was taken to the hospital with a knee injury.

Saturday brought a prediction for a high temperature of fifty degrees. Roads were still slick, but the snow was beginning to melt. Ryan and a friend drove to the mall to pick up suits for the grooms-men. Deep, icy slush covered the parking lot. The only reason the store was open was because two wedding parties had rented tuxedos and suits for Saturday. Ryan could not help laughing when his friend growled a line from a Billy Idol song: "It's a nice day for a white wedding."

In her dressing room at the country club, Anne held a cell phone to one ear and gave directions to guests as her bridesmaids did her hair, makeup, and nails (no beauty shops were open). Everyone who was absolutely necessary made it to the ceremony that afternoon, but many people got lost and either did not get there at all or arrived late. The words on the cover of the wedding program seemed particularly appropriate: "Love bears all things, believes all things, hopes all things, endures all things."

The title of one of Shakespeare's plays might have also come to mind: *All's Well That Ends Well*. "I thought everything turned out wonderful the day of the wedding," Anne said.

According to the National Climatic Data Center, the snowstorm tied for third place in Charlotte's record book with a storm that occurred from February 15 to 17, 1969. The amount of snowfall for each was 13.2 inches. First place still belonged to a storm that dumped 17.4 inches of snow on Charlotte between February 14 and 17, 1902. March 1 and 2, 1927 still held second place with 13.3 inches.

On Sunday the *Charlotte Observer* reported: "Today's highs are expected to reach the mid sixties, and temperatures could reach into the seventies by midweek." The last verse of Tomlinson's poem was right on:

> By week's end the sun will return and re-shine,
> The snow and the salt will have mixed into brine,
> The struggles will fade into memories divine,
> And to think that we saw it in old Caroline!

"Blame it on the weather guys," suggested reporter Huntley. "They never get it right. And even when they do, we don't believe them."

Bibliography

Fayetteville Is No More:
The Great Fire (1831)

"Editor's Correspondence." *The Frederick Town Herald,* Frederick, Md., August 6, 1831, p. 2.

"Fire at Fayetteville." *The Frederick Town Herald,* Frederick, Md., June 18, 1831, p. 3.

"Fire at Fayetteville." *Raleigh Register,* June 2, 1831, p. 2.

"Great Fire at Fayetteville, N.C." *The Adams Sentinel,* Gettysburg, June 7, 1831, p. 3.

Historic Fayetteville and Cumberland County. 1975 Provisional Class of The Junior Service League of Fayetteville. Highland Printers, 1976.

"Historical Highlights." Fayetteville Area Convention and Visitor's Bureau Web site: www.visitfayettevillenc.com.

"Our Town." *The Journal,* Fayetteville, N.C., July 7, 1831, p. 2.

Rowland, Henry A. *The Real Glory of a Church: A Dedication Sermon . . . to which is Appended an Account of the Destruction of Fayetteville.* New York: Jonathan Leavitt and John P. Haven, 1832. Electronic edition accessed at the University of North Carolina at Chapel Hill Libraries Web site, "Documenting the American South," http://docsouth.unc.edu.

Spirit of Cumberland. Published by The Junior Service League of Fayetteville, illustrated by Dan Currie, M.D. Highland Printers, Inc., 1970.

Remember My Last Words:
The Wreck of the Steam Packet *Home* (1837)

Croom, John H., III. "Hardy Bryan Croom: A Man of Means, Talent and History." Croom Family Web site: www.johncroom.com.

Gentile, Gary. *Shipwrecks of North Carolina from Hatteras Inlet South.* Philadelphia: Gary Gentile Productions, 1992.

Hause, Eric. "The Wreck of the *Home,*" CoastalGuide's *Packet* Web site: www.coastalguide.com/packet/homewreck.htm.

Howland, S. A. *Steamboat Disasters and Railroad Accidents in the United States.* Worcester, Mass.: Dorr, Howland, 1840.

Mobley, Joe A. *Ship Ashore! The U.S. Lifesavers of Coastal North Carolina.* Raleigh: Division of Archives and History, North Carolina Department of Cultural Resources, 1994.

"Most Melancholy Disaster!" *The Republican Compiler,* October 24, 1837, p. 4.

Nirenstein, Virginia King. *With Kindly Voices: A Nineteenth-Century Georgia Family.* Macon, Ga.: Tullous Books, 1984.

Stick, David. *Graveyard of the Atlantic.* Chapel Hill, N.C.: The University of North Carolina Press, 1952.

Wilkes, Donald E., Jr. "The Eponymous Mr. Prince." *Flagpole* Magazine Online: www.fairmontfair.com/flagpole/weekly/articles.php?fp=4484.

Tragedy of Errors: The Wreck of the *Metropolis* (1878)

"The Feeling at Philadelphia," *New York Times,* February 2, 1878, p. 1.

Gentile, Gary. *Shipwrecks of North Carolina from the Diamond Shoals North.* Philadelphia: Gary Gentile Productions, 1993.

"Loss of the Steamer *Metropolis.*" *Executive Documents of the House of Representatives for the Second Session of the Forty-Fifth Congress, 1877–'78,* Volume XIV, nos. 34 to 72, except nos. 39, 51, and 61. Washington, D.C.: Government Printing Office, 1878.

Means, Dennis R. "A Heavy Sea Running: The Formation of the U.S. Life-Saving Service, 1846–1878." *Prologue,* A Quarterly Publication of the National Archives and Records Administration, Winter 1987, Vol. 19, No. 4: www.archives.gov/publications/prologue/winter_1987_us_life_saving_service_2.html.

Means, Dennis R. "The Wreck of the *Metropolis.*" *Ibid.*

Mobley, Joe A. *Ship Ashore! The U.S. Lifesavers of Coastal North Carolina.* Raleigh: Division of Archives and History, North Carolina Department of Cultural Resources, 1994.

"The Rotten *Metropolis,*" *New York Times*, February 3, 1878, p. 1.

Sharpe, Bill. "The Catastrophe That Shook America and Led to Establishment of All-Year Beach Control by Our Coast Guard." *The State,* November 3, 1951.

Stick, David. *Graveyard of the Atlantic.* Chapel Hill, N.C.: The University of North Carolina Press, 1952.

"A Terrible Loss of Life," *New York Times,* February 1, 1878, p. 1.

"Wreck of the *Metropolis,*" *New York Tribune,* February 1, 1878, p. 1.

A Frightful Accident:
The Wreck at Bostian Bridge (1891)

Advertisement by Statesville Development Company. *The Landmark.* August 20, 1891.

"A Frightful Accident," *The Landmark.* August 27, 1891.

Gilbert, John F. *Crossties Through Carolina: The Story of North Carolina's Early Day Railroads.* Raleigh: Helios Press, 1969.

Keever, Homer. "Editor J. P. Caldwell's Story of Bostian Bridge Train Wreck in 1891 Is Considered a Classic." *Statesville Record & Landmark,* August 25, 1966.

Lackey, Mac, Jr. "Accounts Recall Horror of Iredell Train Disaster." *Charlotte Observer* (Iredell Neighbors section), in four parts: September 9, 16, 23, and 30, 1987.

The Landmark articles, August 28 and 31 and September 3, 1891.

"Man In Bostian's Bridge Wreck Recalls Statesville As He Knew In That Day, August 27, 1891." *The Landmark,* February 6, 1937.

"Mystery, Notoriety Surround Bostian Train Wreck." *Statesville Record and Landmark,* August 25, 1991.

Roberts, Nancy. *This Haunted Southland, Where Ghosts Still Roam.* Columbia: University of South Carolina Press, 1988.

Tomlin, Jimmy. "Engine No. 9's Ghostly Return Fails to Occur." *Statesville Record & Landmark,* August 27, 1991.

Death of a Dream:
The Hotel Zinzendorf Fire (1892)

Brownlee, Fambrough L. *Winston-Salem: A Pictorial History*. Norfolk, Va.: Donning Co., 1977.

East, Bill. "Big Resort Hotel Had Short Life . . .". *Twin City Sentinel,* Winston-Salem, N.C., November 28, 1956.

——. "Do You Remember . . .". *Twin City Sentinel,* Winston-Salem, N.C., April 6, 1960.

——. "Do You Remember . . .". *Twin City Sentinel,* Winston-Salem, N.C., November 23, 1960.

——. "First Zinzendorf Destroyed by Fire in 1892." *Twin City Sentinel,* Winston-Salem, N.C., November 23, 1971.

——. "Resort Dream Was Short-Lived." *Twin City Sentinel,* Winston-Salem, N.C., November 23, 1967.

"Fire! Fire!" *The People's Press,* Salem, N.C., December 1, 1892, p. 3.

"Hotel Zinzendorf." *The People's Press,* Salem, N.C., October 9, 1890, p. 3.

"Stevenson Gets a Rabbit's Foot." *The Olean Democrat,* Olean, N.Y., September 20, 1892.

Tursi, Frank. *Winston-Salem: A History.* Winston-Salem, N.C.: J. F. Blair, 1994.

"A Typical Summer Home Is The Zinzendorf." *The People's Press,* Salem, N.C., May 26, and June 2, 9, and 16, 1892.

Wellman, Manly Wade, Larry E. Tise, et al. *Winston-Salem in History.* Winston-Salem, N.C.: Historic Winston, 1966–1977.

West End Association Web site: http://thewestend.tripod.com/.

A Wall of Water:
The San Ciriaco Hurricane (1899)

Barnes, Jay. *North Carolina's Hurricane History*. Chapel Hill, N.C.: University of North Carolina Press, 1995, 1998.

"Jug Carried the Rope Ashore and the Crew Was Saved." *The Landmark* (Statesville, N.C.), November 10, 1899, p. 1.

Mobley, Joe A. *Ship Ashore! The U.S. Lifesavers of Coastal North Carolina*. Raleigh: Division of Archives and History, North Carolina Department of Cultural Resources, 1994.

"Porto [*sic*] Rico Tornado." *The Daily Republican,* Decatur, Ill., August 10, 1899, p. 1.

"Rasmus S. Midgett's Gold Lifesaving Medal Rescue." U.S. Coast Guard Web site: www.uscg.mil.

Stick, David. *Graveyard of the Atlantic: Shipwrecks of the North Carolina Coast*. Chapel Hill, N.C.: The University of North Carolina Press, 1952.

"West Indian Wind Storm Playing Out." *The Atlanta Constitution,* August 14, 1899, p. 1.

Williamson, Sonny. *Sailing with Grandpa*. Marshallberg, N.C.: Grandma Publications, 1987.

Two Beasts in Deadly Combat: The Wild West Show Train Wreck (1901)

"Buffalo Bill Is in Town." *Charlotte News,* October 28, 1901.

"Buffalo Bill's Train Damaged—A Collision Between Two Sections with an Exciting Buffalo Hunt Afterward." *The Mansfield News,* Mansfield, Ohio, June 8, 1901, p. 2.

Charlotte Daily Observer articles, October 26, 27, 28, 29, and 30, 1901.

Flory, Claude R. "Annie Oakley in the South." *The North Carolina Historical Review,* Volume XLIII, No. 3, July 1966.

"The Graveyard Express." *Homespun,* edited by Richard Lane and Betty Sowers, October 1974 (a newsletter article based on an interview with Mrs. Annie Lee Sink, daughter of Minnie Young Fitzgerald).

Kasper, Shirl. *Annie Oakley*. Norman: University of Oklahoma Press, 1992.

Riley, Glenda. *The Life and Legacy of Annie Oakley*. Norman: University of Oklahoma Press, 1994.

Scarborough, Franklin. "Did You Hear About Buffalo Bill's 'Wild West Show'?" *Salisbury Post,* September 4, 2000 (in which is reproduced an article by Bob Cloaninger, originally published in the 1960s).

"Two Freight Trains Collide—Col. Cody's Show Train in the Wreck . . .". *The Dispatch,* Lexington, N.C., October 30, 1901.

"Wild West Show Train Wrecked." *The Landmark,* Statesville, N.C., November 1, 1901, p. 1.

Other sources on Annie Oakley in which the incident is mentioned:

Cooper, Courtney Ryley. *Annie Oakley: Woman at Arms.* New York: Duffield and Company, 1927.

Havighurst, Walter. *Annie Oakley of the Wild West.* London: Robert Hale Limited, 1955.

Leader, Glenn Charles, III. "Annie Oakley in Performance: The Evolution of an Image." A Dissertation submitted to the Florida State University School of Theatre, 1997.

Sayers, Isabelle S. *Annie Oakley and Buffalo Bill's Wild West.* Mineola, N.Y.: Dover Publications, Inc., 1981.

Caught in the Middle:
The July Floods (1916)

Arthur, Billy. "The Legacy of Colonel Olds." *The State,* Vol. 56, Issue 11, April 1989, pp. 14–17.

The Asheville Citizen. July 17 and July 19, 1916. Numerous articles.

Brower, Nancy. "The Great Flood." *Asheville Times,* July 9, 1976.

The Floods of July 1916. J. C. Williams, ed. Copyright 1917 by Southern Railway Company. Reprinted 1995 by The Overmountain Press, Johnston City, Tenn.

Green, Lewis. "Saturday Marked 50th Anniversary of Great 1916 Flood." *Asheville Citizen-Times,* July 17, 1966.

Leslie, Lyn. "Flood of 1916 Changed Biltmore Village and Family Lives Forever." Asheville.com, copyright 2003. www.asheville.com/news/.

McJunkin, Cathy. "70 Years Ago, Asheville Felt the Ravages of its Worst Flood in History." *Asheville Citizen-Times,* July 13, 1986.

Olds, Fred. "Marooned in Asheville: A Story of the Great Flood." Date and source unknown. Photocopy provided by Pack Memorial Library, Asheville, N.C.

Reinhardt, Susan. "Victim of the flood of 1916 never forgot." *Asheville Citizen-Times,* September 9, 2004: www.citizen-times.com.

Killer on the Loose:
The Influenza Pandemic (1918)

Charlotte Observer articles, October and November 1918.

Cockrell, David L. "A Blessing in Disguise: The Influenza Pandemic of 1918 and North Carolina's Medical and Public Health Communities." *The North Carolina Historical Review,* Vol. LXXIII, No. 3, July 1996. Copyright 1996, North Carolina Division of Archives and History.

Crosby, Alfred W. *America's Forgotten Pandemic: The Influenza of 1918.* New York: Cambridge University Press, 1989.

Joseph B. Mathews Papers, 1917–1919. University of North Carolina at Charlotte Manuscript Collection 252, J. Murrey Atkins Library.

Mitchell, Miriam Grace and Edward Spaulding Perzel. *The Echo of the Bugle Call: Charlotte's Role in World War I.* Charlotte, N.C.: Dowd House Preservation Committee; Citizens for Preservation, Inc., 1979.

Morrill, Dan L. *Historic Charlotte: An Illustrated History of Charlotte and Mecklenburg County.* Published by Historic Charlotte, Inc., in cooperation with Historical Publishing Network, a division of Lammert Publications, Inc., San Antonio, 2001.

Presbyterial Hospital: The Spirit of Caring, 1903–1985. Dallas: Taylor Publishing Company, 1991.

Strong, Dr. Charles M. *History of Mecklenburg County Medicine.* Charlotte, N.C.: [S.l. : s.n.], News Printing House, 1929.

No Use Being Sorrowful:
The Coal Glen Mine Disaster (1925)

Cecelski, David. "Margaret Wicker: The Coal Glen Mine Disaster," as published in the February 13, 2000, edition of the *Raleigh News & Observer:* http://freepages.history.rootsweb.com/~pfwilson/coal_glen .html.

Charlotte Observer articles, May 28, 29, 30, and 31, 1925.

Clement, Melissa. "Mine explosion victims remembered," Fayetteville Online, 2000. http://freepages.history.rootsweb.com/~pfwilson /coal_glen.html.

"Coal Glen Mine Gives Up Dead." *Chatham Record,* June 4, 1925, p. 1.

"The Coal Glen Mining Disaster" Web site. Material compiled by Paul F. Wilson. http://freepages.history.rootsweb.com/-pfwilson/coal_glen.html.

"Coal Glen Now Desolate After Its Great Tragedy." *Sanford Express,* June 5, 1925.

Drye, Willie. "Mine Field." *Our State,* August 1999, pp. 70–75.

Durham Morning Herald articles, May 28, 29, 30, and 31 and June 1 and 2, 1925.

Fayetteville Observer articles, May 28, 29, and 30, and June 1, 1925.

Hetzer, Michael. "The Coal Demon of Deep River." *The State Magazine,* June 1987, pp. 14–17.

"Little Hope Left for Rescue of Any of Entombed Miners Alive." *The Sanford Express,* May 29, 1925, p. 1.

Raleigh News & Observer articles, May 27, 29, 30, and 31, and June 1, 1925.

Thirty-Fifth Report of the Department of Labor and Printing of the State of North Carolina, 1925–1926. Chapter VI: Mines and Mining. Frank D. Grist, Commissioner. Mitchell Printing Company: Raleigh, 1926.

Gathering Storm:
The August Floods (1940)

Greene, Mrs. Ivery C. *A Disastrous Flood: A True and Fascinating Story.* Copyright 1941 by Mrs. Ivery C. Greene, Deep Gap, N.C.

Greene, James C. Telephone interview, January 20, 2005.

The Heritage of Watauga County, North Carolina, Volume I. Published by The Heritage of Watauga County Book Committee in cooperation with Hunter Publishing Company. Winston-Salem, 1984.

The Heritage of Watauga County, North Carolina, Volume II. Edited by Curtis Smalling. Winston-Salem: Hunter Publishing Company, 1987.

"16 Dead in Floods; South's Loss Heavy." *New York Times,* August 15, 1940, p. 24.

"Sixteen Wataugans Lose Lives as Flood Waters Sweep Over County." *Watauga Democrat,* August 22, 1940.

"Survivors of August Floods Describe Deep Gap Tragedy." *Watauga Democrat,* September 19, 1940, p. 6.

"Three Perish in Flood: Death Toll Mounts in Appalling Disaster." *Watauga Democrat,* August 15, 1940.

Like a Bad Dream:
The Atlantic Coast Line Wreck (1943)

Atlantic Coast Line Wreck, December 16, 1943, Lumberton, N.C. Official Report of Relief Operations. Washington, D.C.: The American National Red Cross, 1944.

Chicago Daily Tribune articles, December 17, 18, 19, and 20, 1943.

Griffin, William E., Jr. *Atlantic Coast Line: Standard Railroad of the South.* Lynchburg, Va.: TLC Publishing Inc., 2001.

"Interstate Commerce Commission - Washington - Investigation No. 2751 - The Atlantic Coast Line Railroad Company Report in re Accident Near Rennert, N.C. on December 16, 1943." Department of Transportation Special Collections Web site: http://dotlibrary.specialcollection.net.

The Robesonian. Lumberton, N.C.: December 16, 17, 20 , 21, and 22, 1943.

St. Louis Post-Dispatch articles, December 16, 17, 18, and 19, 1943.

"Surrender Touches Off Wild Celebration in City." *St. Petersburg Times,* August 15, 1945. University of South Florida Digital Collections Web site: www.lib.usf.edu/ldsu/digitalcollections.

Wilkins, Tim. "Blood on the Tracks." *The Robesonian,* Lumberton, N.C., December 16, 2003. www.robesonian.com.

Princess in a Tower:
The Highland Hospital Fire (1948)

"Bodies of Two More Victims of Fire Found." *Asheville Citizen,* March 13, 1948.*

Cline, Sally. *Zelda Fitzgerald: Her Voice in Paradise.* New York: Arcade Publishing, 2002.

"Highland Night Nurse Testifies in Fire Inquest." *Asheville Times,* March 26, 1948.*

"Hospital Fire Jury Finds No Criminal Blame." *Asheville Citizen,* April 1, 1948.*

"Hospital Staff Members and 2 Youths Praised." *Asheville Times,* March 12, 1948.*

Miller, L. P. "Strange, Human Stories Come from Big Fire." *Asheville Times,* March 12, 1948.*

"Miss Hall to Enter Hospital." *Asheville Citizen*, April 17, 1948.*

Padgitt, Bright W. "Nine Women Die in Fire at Highland Hospital." *Asheville Times,* March 11, 1948.*

Taylor, Kendall. *Sometimes Madness Is Wisdom (Zelda and Scott Fitzgerald: A Marriage)*. New York: Ballantine Books, 2001.

* Page numbers for articles in *Asheville Times* and *Asheville Citizen* are not known. Articles were copied from library clippings file.

Everything Was Just Gone: Hurricane Hazel (1954)

Barnes, Jay. *North Carolina's Hurricane History.* Chapel Hill: University of North Carolina Press, 1998.

Cantwell, Si. "Ocean Isle Beach family perishes in Hazel's arms." *Wilmington Star-News,* October 9, 2004. www.starnewsonline.com.

———. "Remembering Hurricane Hazel 50 Years Later." *Ibid.*

Drye, Willie. "Worst Hurricane in North Carolina: 50 Years Later." http://news.nationalgeographic.com.

"Elderly Lady Was Heroine." *Statesville Record & Landmark,* February 25, 1955, p. 10.

"1953 Hurricane/Tropical Data for Atlantic," Unisys Weather Web site (data provided from the National Weather Service via the NOAAPORT satellite data service). http://weather.unisys.com/hurricane/atlantic/1953/index.html.

Seamon, L. H. "The Storm of October 15, 1954." Reprinted from U.S. Department of Commerce, Weather Bureau's Climatological Data, National Summary, Vol. 5, No. 10, 1954.

Shaw, Matt. "Residents Remember Hurricane Hazel." *Goldsboro News-Argus,* October 10, 2004. www.newsargus.com.

"U.S. Weather Bureau Log." *Wilmington Star-News,* October 9, 2004. www.starnewsonline.com.

Waggoner, Martha. "Fifty years later, Hazel remains high-water mark for Carolina hurricanes." Copyright 2004, The Associated Press. www.lancasteronline.com.

Yancey, Noel. "Graham Has Job He Wanted at Time He Was a 10-Year-Old Boy." *Burlington (N.C.) Daily Times-News,* October 10, 1964.

Fallout from a Cold War:
The Crashes of Two B-52 Bombers (1961)

"Big AF Plane Crashes; One Known Dead." *Greensboro Daily News,* March 31, 1961, p. 1.

"Broken Arrow: Goldsboro, N.C." A semester project undertaken by four students at the University of North Carolina at Chapel Hill. Posted at ibiblio.org (a collaboration of the Center for the Public Domain and The University of North Carolina Chapel Hill): www.ibiblio.org/bomb.

Burchette, Bob. "Disaster in Denton." *Greensboro News & Record,* March 28, 2003, p. D1.

———. "Residents Recall Crash of B-52." *Greensboro News & Record,* March 31, 2003, p. B3.

"Huge Bomber Crashes; 3 Are Killed." *Greensboro Daily News,* January 25, 1961, p. 1.

"Life-Death Story of Flight Told." *Greensboro Daily News,* January 26, 1961, p. B4.

"Many Flock to Scene of Crash" and "Officer Aboard Fatal Plane Relates Escape by Parachute." *Greensboro Daily News,* April 1, 1961, pp. 1 and 7.

"McNamara recalls nuclear near hits." *Daily Herald* (Chicago), September 16, 1983, p. 11.

Utting, Gerald. "Will accidents trigger nuclear Armageddon?" *Lethbridge Herald,* Alberta, Canada, October 17, 1983.

Womick, Chip. "B-52 Crash remembered." *Courier-Tribune,* Asheboro, N.C., March 17, 2003.

Terrain! Terrain!
The Crash of Flight 1016 (1994)

"Aircraft Accident Report: Flight into Terrain during Missed Approach; USAir Flight 1016, DC-9-31, N954VJ, Charlotte-Douglas International Airport, Charlotte, North Carolina, July 2, 1994." Washington, D.C.: National Transportation Safety Board.

Charlotte Observer articles, July 3–10, 1994.

Chicago Tribune articles, July 3, 5, and 6, 1994.

"Consistent Use of 'Silent Review' Supports Quick, Correct Actions." *Flight Safety Foundation Cabin Crew Safety,* Vol. 37, No. 2, March–April 2002.

Garfield, Ken. "Memorial Honors the Dead, the Rescuers from USAir Crash." *Charlotte Observer,* February 25, 1996, p. 1B.

On a Wing and a Prayer: Interviews with Airline Disaster Survivors. Edited by Malcolm MacPherson. New York: Perennial, an Imprint of Harper-Collins Publishers, 2002.

Paulsen, Monte. "Charlotte pilots recount last moments." *The State,* July 6, 1994.

"Sudden Impact—A Flight Attendant's Story of Courage and Survival." By Editorial Staff with Richard DeMary. *Flight Safety Foundation Cabin Crew Safety,* Vol. 30, No. 2, March–April 1995; and Vol. 30, No. 3, May–June 1995.

A Risky Business:
The Speedway Disaster (2000)

The Charlotte Observer articles from May, June, and November 2000: www.charlotte.com.

CNN, various articles, May 2000. www.cnn.com.

CNN/*Sports Illustrated,* various articles, May 2000. http://sports illustrated.cnn.com.

Hunter, Don and Al Pearce. *The Illustrated History of Stock Car Racing.* Osceola, Wis.: MBI Publishing Company, 1998.

Lowe's Motor Speedway Web site. www.lowesmotorspeedway.com.

Menzer, Joe. *The Wildest Ride: A History of NASCAR.* New York: Simon & Schuster, 2001.

NASCAR: The Thunder of America. New York: HarperHorizon ("A Tehabi Book"), 1998.

"Newton man, winner of NASCAR's first stock car race, dead at age of 83." *Lawrence Journal-World,* June 25, 2000. www.ljworld.com.

"Some still haunted year after walkway collapse." *The Star,* May 21, 2001. www.shelbystar.com.

White Wedding, Black Ice:
The February Snowstorm (2004)

The Charlotte Observer (various articles). February 26–29, 2004. www .charlotte.com/mld/charlotte.

Huntley, Dan. "We Doubters Are Awash in White Stuff." *Charlotte Observer,* February 27, 2004. www.charlotte.com/mld/charlotte.

Kelley, Anne Baltz. E-mail correspondence, May 2004.

Kelley, Ryan. E-mail correspondence, May 2004.

"More black ice expected overnight." News 14 Carolina and Associated Press, February 28, 2004. www.news14charlotte.com.

"Selected U.S. City and State Extremes, February 2004." compiled by NCDC (source: NOAA/NWS Forecast Offices). www.ncdc.noaa.gov.

Tomlinson, Tommy. "From Bad to Verse: Snow Brings Out Poet in a Parka." *Charlotte Observer* (Metro Section), February 27, 2004, p. 1B. www.charlotte.com/mld/charlotte.

WSOC-TV Web site (various articles). February 25–27, 2004. www.wsoctv.com.

About the Author

Scotti McAuliff Cohn is a freelance writer and copy editor specializing in health care and history. A former resident of Asheville, North Carolina, she now resides in Bloomington, Illinois, with her husband and three cats. She has written four other books for The Globe Pequot Press: *More Than Petticoats: Remarkable North Carolina Women; It Happened in North Carolina; Beyond Their Years: Stories of Sixteen Civil War Children;* and *Liberty's Children: Stories of Eleven Revolutionary War Children.*

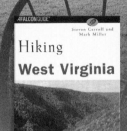
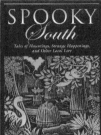

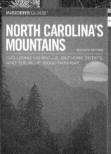